Copyright © 2023 Randall Niznick

All rights reserved

No part of this book may be reproduced, or stored in a retrieval system, or transmitted in any form or by any means, electronic, mechanical, photocopying, recording, or otherwise, without express written permission of the publisher.

ISBN: 9798863929705

Cover design by: Robert Harrison
Library of Congress Control Number: 2018675309
Printed in the United States of America

To Sheri, you are my rock. Thank you for your love and support. I would not be half the person I am today if it were not for you, I love you!

Contents

Copyright
Dedication
Preface
Ch.1: Deciding to Join the Navy 1
Ch.2: The US Navy...My Early Career Days 20
Ch.3: The Cheeseburger Incident 29
Ch.4: Transfer To The US Navy Seabees 36
Ch.5: Haitian and Cuban Migration Of 1994 54
Ch.6: Recruiting Scandal 61
Ch.7: Meeting "The One" 67
Ch.8: Making Chief Petty Officer 77
Ch.9: 2004 Indian Ocean Tsunami 84
Ch.10: Never Give Up On Those You Lead 95
Ch.11: US Naval Academy 99
Ch.12: Naval Support Unit, US Department of State 107
Diplomatic Security
Ch.13: Transition To Civilian World 122

Ch. 14: Fatherhood	148
Words of Wit	159
Acknowledgements	161
About The Author	163
Disclaimer	167
References	169
My Military Career Timeline	171
My Military Retirement Speech Manuscript	173

Preface

I feel too many veterans stories are lost because they are not put into writing and not properly documented. We (veterans) have a story and it is a story worth sharing! If anything, it is a story worth sharing for our family and all future generations to come. It is my number one desire in writing this book to capture my life and more specifically, my military service, so that future generations of my family will always have something to read, reflect upon, and maybe share a laugh or tear with.

Secondly, I wanted to write this book to show gratitude to everyone in my life, especially my wife Sheri. I cannot express enough in words the love I have for Sheri. She has and will always remain my rock. She has made me who I am today, and I am forever grateful. In addition to Sheri, there have been many who have given me advice, set me straight, or just given me wise counsel and for that I am forever indebted.

This is also for my fellow veterans, especially my fellow Enlisted veterans. We have all had our challenges in service to our country, but perhaps one of the biggest challenges we all face is adjusting to civilian life post-military. It is my hope that in the chapter where I speak to my own transition I am able to help my fellow veterans in theirs.

Lastly, this is for anyone who is just starting out in "adulting" and entering corporate life. I willingly share some leadership lessons (good and bad) to demonstrate that life is but a journey of learning and that there will be times you work for good leaders and times you work for bad ones. It is how you react to those leaders or situations that will make you who you aspire to be.

This book has some very emotional chapters. I forewarn the reader, some of the content gets a bit graphic. But it is necessary to set the tone and put the reader into the situation as best as possible. It is my ultimate desire that whoever reads this book develops a better understanding of what it means to serve, no matter what the capacity. I also hope that perhaps this book will give you the spark to embark on your own life of service! In so doing, we can all do our part to make this world just a little bit better.

Ch.1: Deciding to Join the Navy

"When you turn 18 you are out of this house and on your own!". This was my wakeup call at around the age of 16 or 17, I do not specifically recall. But I knew I had to figure out "life" and I did not have a lot of time to do it!

But before I take you into my journey of joining the United States Navy Seabees, I want to take you back to my childhood and talk a little about my upbringing.

First, let me say that I come from divorced parents. I was about age 9 when my parents divorced from what I recollect. I do not remember much of my early childhood years with my father as he was an alcoholic and was in a constant state of drunkenness. What I do remember is the *hell* my mom went through dealing with his alcoholism, raising three sons, and working her butt off to make ends meet. I also remember the numerous times we found ourselves with little to no money because my father would spend it all on alcohol and cigarettes.

My mom was the rock that kept our family together.

Prior to his falling apart, my father worked at the local Cleveland, Ohio newspaper as a cartoonist from what I recall. However, he was laid off and that was what sent him into the downward spiral of alcoholism. Due to the lay off and subsequent alcoholism, my mom was forced to go to work so we could continue to have an income. My mom worked two jobs just to keep the bills paid and us three boys were left to our own accord going through school. I remember seeing my mom Monday through Friday only briefly, in-between her day job and her night job. All in all, it was usually about an hour in early evening that we would see each other during the weekdays. But most times, my mom would leave us boys' food in the fridge that we would reheat on our own for dinner.

I struggled in my early years of school because of the situation at home. I remember skipping school a lot. Now mind you, this was like the fourth or fifth grade, I do not specifically recollect, but I was young, very young. I just had no direction and quite frankly, did not care much about school. I was more into smoking cigarettes and just hanging out with the wrong crowd. I was never into sports or anything like that, I was into music and just getting into trouble more than anything. And you may wonder how a kid my age was able to get cigarettes. Well, back in the day, cigarettes were not behind the counter but rather they were right there in the aisles. It was pretty easy for me to just steal packs of cigarettes as I needed them.

My mom had warned my dad numerous times that if he did not get a hold of his drinking problem, she would leave him and take us kids with her. I vaguely remember the one time he actually tried to quit drinking. It did not last long and before too long he was putting whiskey in his coffee. I remember this because I would smell it on his breath. Nothing like the smell of whiskey and coffee first thing in the morning and then be told "I haven't been drinking son". Ya right, ok..., you are full of crap, but ok.

This struggle with alcohol and my dad went on for a long while. After too many open promises of "I will quit drinking", my mom decided she had enough and filed for divorce. I must have been around 8 years old or so. I vaguely remember how this all went down or my age at the time but I do remember the fights, they got pretty bad at times.

I remember how I would just bury my head in my pillow on my bed and rock back and forth while humming to myself. This was my coping mechanism to block out the sounds of my dad physically abusing my mom. I believe when my mom finally had enough she kicked him out of the house and he went to live with his mother. Honestly, I do not remember much of this part of my childhood as I have permanently suppressed that part of my life from memory.

And so my mom was now a single parent, left to bring up three boys on her own. She worked tirelessly to keep the bills paid, a roof over our head, lights on, and food on the table. I remember we were on food stamps to help stretch the dollar a bit more. I also remember our electricity being turned off for non-payment of bill on numerous occasions. Yes, back in the day, public utilities would turn off services for non-payment without hesitation. I do not think that happens much these days, thank goodness.

It was at the job my mom worked during the day that she met Ron. As I understand it, they would talk just about weekly, I think he ordered parts from a store she worked at or something, I do not really know. But he saw how tired she was, and he knew she was struggling to make ends meet. When I look at some of those photos of my mom back then I can now see the exhaustion in her eyes. It is amazing how we see things with a different lens when we look back on childhood photos as an adult.

I never realized at the time how little sleep my mom was actually getting, I do not know how she did it honestly.

I do not remember the specific day or instance when my mom introduced us three boys to her new boyfriend (who would eventually end up being our stepfather). I personally did not even know my mom was dating again honestly. But those introductions were made and as far as I remember, us boys were happy for mom.

After some time had passed and things were getting more serious, my mom decided we were going to move in with Ron. I am sure he saw her struggling to pay bills and make the mortgage and was the one who initiated the idea, but I cannot say for sure because I was not witness to those conversations.

What I do know is this was a turning point in my childhood and a massive wake up call. Up to this point, I had no discipline and I mean that literally. I was pretty much living on my own and free to do what I wanted because my mom was too busy working those two jobs. We (the boys) had the run of the house for the most part. But that was soon to change and change drastically.

Ron was a strict stepfather who believed strongly in discipline and respect for your parents. At the beginning, this was a rough thing for me to understand and accept. I never had rules or chores, I freely went about my days doing what I had wished. I also played drums and jammed a lot with my best friend who to this day is a very talented singer and musician. He is one of those people that can pick up just about any instrument and in about 1 to 2 weeks will know how to play it and play it well!

But I digress.

I remember when we started going over to Ron's home. I was awestruck by the house.., in my eyes it was like a mansion! The house we lived in prior to the move was very small and not in the best part of town. We were now living in a middle to upper class neighborhood and the houses were beautiful! I never experienced this kind of living and it was completely different than what I was used to.

I remember that first time seeing the house, I turned and looked at my mom and said, "we are rich, mom!" You have to remember I was extremely young and never had experienced anything like this. Heck, my mom made our clothes! I remember many times going to JoAnn Fabrics to look at patterns and pick out the pants and shirts I wanted my mom to make for me. And let us not forget my earlier mention of electricity being turned off for non-payment. And now, we were moving into this home that was seemingly (at least in the eyes of a little kid) twice the size and just simply gorgeous as opposed to what I had been used to.

Ron was a strict disciplinarian and put his foot down from day one. It was apparent he saw that us three boys were very independent and made our own rules and he was quick to put an end to all of it. I vaguely remember some of our disagreements and how I would lose my temper and storm out of the house. I would say something like "that is it, I am booking!" and off I would go, out the front door and partially down the street. Needless to say I never made it very far. Ron would snatch me up and bring me back into the house where he would then proceed to tell me things like "this is my house, and as long as you are living under my roof, you will play by my rules." It took me several years to embrace this new father figure in my life and his strict ways but once I did, things improved for me.

We were a blue-collar family through and through. My stepfather was the Maintenance Director for a Tool and Die/Press Stampings plant back in Ohio. He was a highly skilled and self taught industrial electrician and welder. In all respects, my stepfather was an absolutely brilliant welder! If there is one thing I wish I would have learned from him it is welding. I never took an interest in it but wish I had, it is a great skill for anyone to have. Ron even taught welding part-time at a technical night school, that was how much he loved this particular trade.

Another fond memory I have of my stepfather was his homemade Christmas light display for our house. He made all the light displays himself, from scratch. He had two large wooden stars made of plywood with different colored incandescent lights wired onto them. He also had this cool Santa Clause that sat atop a rocketship. The flames coming off the back of the rocketship were multi-colored synchronized lights.

Now, how he got each decoration to have synchronized lighting is a bit of an old school electrical feat. He had numerous old traffic light controllers (Lord knows where he obtained them all from)! All the wires from each outdoor light decoration would be pulled into the basement of our house. In the basement, Ron had a large folding table set up with all these traffic controller motors on top. He would meticulously wire each motor to each set of colored lights that were on a display. It is hard to explain but these motors basically had a rotating cam that would strike against an individual contact. Once the cam hit the contact, that would close the electrical circuit for that particular set of lights.

So for example, the star. The star had an outline of red lights, then blue lights, yellow lights, etcetera. As each contact was hit by the cam, that sequence of lights would illuminate. This was way before computers so this was the way my stepfather knew to make the lights flicker and do various patterns. It was really ingenious when I think back to it all. I remember hearing all those motors clicking and seeing the small blue arcing as the contacts were quickly electrified to send the signal to the fixture outside. Was it the most electrically safe and OSHA compliant installation??? Ummm, I plead the fifth.

But every year us boys would help set up this pretty sizeable (at least back in the day) Christmas display. One year we even won Christmas Display of the year by our local town. Ron received a nice plaque that he hung on the wall next to the wet bar we had in our living room. I still remember that plaque to this day. It was pretty cool to see him receive it considering all the hard work it took to put the display together. Helping Ron with all the electrical connections was just another way he taught me electricity and how motors and controllers worked, life lessons that I have never forgotten.

College was never spoken of in our home nor did my parents save any money for any of us kids to attend college. We were raised to work with our hands and learn a trade. I remember learning the basics of auto care like changing oil, replacing brakes, gapping spark plugs, etc... from my stepdad. Ron was a Mopar or No Car guy and owned a 1970 Dodge Polara with a 440 cubic inch engine. That car was his pride and joy albeit a "boat". If anyone knows about the Dodge Polara, you know how big that car is! He also owned a Dodge Charger but sold it early on when we moved in with him so I vaguely remember that car.

My stepdad would always bring us kids under the hood with him whenever he was tinkering. I remember him showing me how to "fine tune" the air-fuel mixture at the carburetor to get it to run at its peak efficiency among many other common mechanical tune ups. He loved that car and loved showing me and my brother how to maintain it, how to tune it, and especially how to drive it! I have many memories of him driving us around on the back roads, top down (it was a convertible) and laying into the throttle. We would get pushed back into our seats as that 440 cubic inch engine worked its magic on the pavement!

At age 14 I started working with my stepdad at the press stampings/tool and die plant. My stepdad believed strongly in teaching work ethic at a young age. I have always appreciated those years I spent working alongside him at the plant. It taught me so much in the way of work ethic and being loyal to a company. Now, I know that last part may seem a bit odd in today's day and age but you must remember, this was the early to mid-eighties where people worked for one company for their entire career!

I was doing really well working at the plant but not all the work was glamourous. I remember performing preventative maintenance on the large Minster presses. This consisted of climbing up to the top and cleaning all the grease from the ram assembly with acetone (not the type of acetone used as a nail polish remover, this stuff was much more potent!). I still remember those fumes of the acetone as it would permeate my nostrils. It would actually make me light-headed and I would have to go outside to get some fresh air! Oh man, the memories.

However, in doing that preventative maintenance work, I will always remember Ron instilling a sense of curiousity into me. He would always tell me that while I am up there cleaning the grease, look at the mechanicals. Really get a sense of how everything works together to drive the ram up and down, etc.. And I would! I would genuinely be curious, taking in all the mechanical and electrical components and gain an understanding of all the intricacies of these massive fabrication machines! To this day, I have an ABL... Always Be Learning mindset. I owe that to Ron and how he always pushed me to look beyond the task at hand and be curious as to how things worked and operated. His wisdom has served me well in my career and otherwise!

The owner (who was also very good friends with my stepdad) took a liking to me. My stepdad told him that I was taking drafting in High School. Back then we had vocational classes that you could choose to take instead of college preparation classes. The owner said he would like for me to shadow their draftsman that worked in the front office. I did not fully understand it at the time but he was wanting to train me up so I could work for the plant as a tool and die draftsman. Once it clicked in my head what he was wanting to do, I got pretty excited. Looking at the mechanical drawings the draftsman would draw was mesmerizing and I really took an interest in it.

But my stepfather, being older and wiser, pulled me aside and said that he did not want me to stay working at the plant. He wanted to see me do something more, get out of Ohio and see the world. This was when he said, "you should join the Navy!".

For context, my stepfather was a US Navy veteran

himself who served in Vietnam. My brother and cousin were currently serving in the US Navy as well. My stepfather continued to press me on joining the Navy. He would tell me sea stories and constantly tell me how joining the Navy was the best thing he ever did. Oh man, the sea stories.., they were always "entertaining"!

So, in retrospect, my future was pretty much already decided. I was going to follow my family in their footsteps and join the Navy! Little did I realize how much this decision would have a profound impact on me and my life.

But before I proceed with that story, I do want to talk about a US Naval incident that occurred that directly hit home with our family.

The day was May 9th, 1989. My mom was watching the evening news when there was breaking news. The newscaster proceeded to say there was an explosion on a US Navy Ship. My mom's ears perked up but since they did not disclose the name of the ship right away, she showed concern but was not overly concerned. But, her concern did quickly turn to fear as they stated the explosion occurred on the USS White Plains. This was the ship my brother (her son) was serving on! My brother was a Machinist Mate Third Class Petty Officer (MM3) at the time and we knew he was at sea doing what the Navy does.

My mom immediately went into panic mode and as

they directed viewers to do on the news, she tried calling the American Red Cross for details. You see, whenever there is an incident like this within the military, the American Red Cross acts as the messengers for families back home. Unfortunately my mom could not get through because the phone lines were so busy with so many people calling for information.

I believe it took about 48 hours before my mom was able to get through to the Red Cross and obtain more detailed information. It was at this time we found out my brother was okay.

As the story goes, there was a fuel oil leak on one of the boilers that immediately ignited and caused an explosion. My brother was in the area when this explosion occurred. I do not know the details but my brother was able to escape the area and survived this tragic accident that killed six of his shipmates.

You may think this incident would have deterred me from wanting to join the Navy but it didn't. I fully understood the dangers that came with serving in the military and I willingly accepted those dangers. It is just what we do as citizens whom want to serve our country in the military, we willingly accept those inherent risks.

***

I will never forget the day I decided to go to the Navy

Recruiting office, it was in my senior year of high school. I am sure the recruiter will never forget it either because it was possibly one of the easiest "sales" he ever closed! I walked into the office and basically said "*I want to join the Navy*"! The recruiters in the office looked at me with a skeptical look. At the time I did not really understand that skepticism (it was not until years later when I was a Navy Recruiter myself that I came to understand why "walk ins" were not always the best candidates for military service). Nonetheless, they sat me down and started telling selling me on Naval service. I stopped them and said, "I know about the Navy, I have family who is serving, just tell me where to sign".

Now, recruiters are smart, and they also value their time with each candidate. Although I was certainly motivated to join, they had to do their due diligence to ensure I would pass the entrance exam. They sat me down and gave me the practice ASVAB in the office to ensure I would be able to make a qualifying score. The ASVAB is short for "Armed Services Vocational Aptitude Battery" test. It is a multiple-choice test that identifies a candidate's strengths so that they can be classified into a rating (job) that they will have the best chance to succeed at. For example, if a candidate scores low on mechanical aptitude, then that individual will not be qualified for any rates that require mechanical skills and understanding (aptitude).

Needless to say I scored well and we scheduled a date

to go to the MEPS (Military Entrance Processing Station) to join the Navy. When a candidate gets a date to go to the MEPS it is quite the "entertaining" ordeal! Most times (and as it was for me), the recruiter will take the candidate the night before their scheduled date. I was put up in a hotel (all expenses paid) and was told to be ready to wake up and go to the MEPS at around 0300 (3:00AM). Truth be told, I vaguely remember my day at the MEPS.

Nonetheless, I do remember the first step of the process, the physical exam. It is here that many feel *"violated"*. I will not get into the details but if you are truly curious, just ask any military veteran about their MEPS physical exam and they will more than likely give you a *very* entertaining account of their experience! After completing the physical exam, I proceeded to the next step of the process, classification.

Classification is when a Navy Classifier sits you down and tells you what rates (jobs) you are qualified to do and that are currently available. I remember this step of the process vaguely, but I do remember one surprising discovery made by the physical exam...I was found to be colorblind! This took me by surprise because I had been working with my stepdad doing high voltage electrical work and never did I have a problem identifying wires by their color. Additionally (and even more discouraging), I wanted to be an electrician in the Navy! With this newfound discovery of colorblindness, I was not eligible for any electrical/electronic/aviation rates and I was frustrated. This was a gut punch and I still remember how my heart sank upon hearing the news that I could not be a "sparky" (slang for electrician).

Be that as it may, the classifier was extremely educated on the rates in the Navy and he also saw the disappointment in my face. He took another hard look at the computer monitor, taking time to review with scrutiny whatever it was he was looking at. After what seemed like an eternity, he looked up from the screen and proceeded to tell me that I could be a Utilitiesman. He told me that as a Utilitiesman I would learn about Air-Conditioning. He proceeded to explain that being an Air-Conditioning technician would afford me the opportunity to work with electricity and electrical components. He explained that the UT (Utilitiesman) rating did not have a color vision requirement, so I was qualified for the rate although I was color blind. With his explanation and also the fact that I always found air-conditioning systems to be interesting, I agreed to sign into the Navy as a UT (Utilitiesman).

The next question was "how soon can you ship to boot camp?". There is always a sense of urgency to get candidates off to boot camp for a myriad of reasons, but perhaps the number one reason is buyer's remorse. Being a former Navy Recruiter and Classifier myself, I know firsthand about this sense of urgency and the importance behind it. But in this instance I was ready to go, so having an early ship date was a non-issue. He asked if August was a good time and I, without hesitation, agreed. So as it were, I would ship to boot camp on August 13, 1990.

When you join the Navy and are assigned a rating, you receive a rate card to take home with you. This rate card explains the rate, where the school is, how long the school is, and some other details of the job. Being young I really did not look at this rate card in finite detail. I just understood that I would be working in the air-conditioning and plumbing trades and I was ecstatic! When I came home from the MEPS my stepdad was sitting in his recliner.

Oh boy, that recliner.., my stepdad loved that recliner! After a hard day at work or a long day of working out in the yard or under the hood of the Dodge he would plop down on his recliner, turn on the television, pour himself an ice cold coca-cola and relax. This day was no different other than the fact he was anxiously awaiting my arrival so he could find out what I would be doing in the Navy. I will never forget the look on his face when he read the rate card and saw in tiny print "Seabees".

I do not know how he saw the word "Seabees" among all the other text on that rate card but when he did, he was overcome with excitement. "Randy, you are going to be a Seabee! Back when I was serving in the Navy *everyone* wanted to be a Seabee"! "You will be able to get out of the Navy and walk *right* into a *great* job out here because being a Seabee will give you skills that are *always* in demand". Like every other 17-year-old kid, I did not really think much about that at the time but hey, it sounded great!

I shipped off to boot camp (Recruit Training Command) at Great Lakes, Illinois on August 13th, 1990 (and also took my first airplane ride, added bonus!).

Boot Camp was an adventure, let me tell you! I will never forget one of the first things that was said to me as I stepped off the bus at O'dark-thirty in the morning. *"Hey big ears, get your ass off the bus and get moving"!* "Welcome to Boot Camp" I said to myself. Despite that first impression, looking back, it was not particularly bad.

I completed boot camp without incident and the foundation of my Naval Service was laid, I was now a sailor in the world's greatest Navy!

Ch.2: The US Navy...My Early Career Days

When I joined the US Navy, I was placed into a pilot enlistment program called Targeted A-School. What this entailed was I had a guaranteed A-School when I signed up at the Military Entrance Processing Station but there would be a delay in when I would attend my A-school. A-School is your initial trade school that teaches you the basics of your rating (trade). However, I was not going to go to A-School immediately upon graduation from Boot Camp as is normally the case. Instead, I would have to wait 12 to 18 months before going to A-School. The reason for this program (as I understand it) was to address a high failure rate at various A-Schools throughout the Navy.

The thought process was to send sailors to the fleet to work in their prospective rate to gain hands on experience. In theory, by having sailors work in their rate and receive on-the-job training for a period of 12 to 18 months, they would have a higher probability of passing A-School. There was one issue with my particular situation (and other prospective Seabees who were placed in this program)..., you cannot go to a Seabee command "undesignated". Undesignated means you joined the Navy but you have not attended and graduated A-School for your particular rating. Because this program sent us to the fleet immediately upon graduation and without attending A-school from boot camp, we were considered undesignated.

But as I previously stated, you cannot go to a Seabee command without already graduating from A-School. So, instead of going to a Seabee Command, we were sent to the fleet Navy as undesignated seamen where we worked in deck division. Deck division is the division that is responsible to maintain and preserve the ship. It is also the division that is responsible for underway replenishments (refueling at sea, receiving stores (goods) at sea, and line-handling when pulling into port or leaving port). The main rate in deck division is Boatswains Mate. So, as it were, I was sent to the fleet reporting to the USS Elrod, FFG-55 home-ported out of Charleston, South Carolina. FFG stands for Fast-Frigate, Guided-Missile.

I do not regret this experience by any means. Although I joined to be a Navy Seabee, I welcomed the opportunity to experience "fleet life"..., also known as "haze gray and underway" like my brother and cousin had. The ship I was assigned was an Oliver Hazard Perry Class Fast Frigate, a small boy in comparison to the majority of US Navy Ships. I will never forget one of the first things told to me when I reported aboard. I was informed that a Fast Frigate was essentially the "bullet catcher" for Aircraft Carriers as it is cheaper to rebuild a Frigate if it gets hit then an Aircraft Carrier. Wow, ok, glad to be onboard I thought to myself.

So there I was, a sailor on a ship. We did a couple short duration deployments in support of drug interdictions and other "enforcement" type activities. These were short underway periods, usually lasting just a few weeks or a month. These shorter duration underway periods keep the crew in practice and kept us trained up for when we would have to embark on the full six to eight month deployments.

Thinking back on these short duration underway periods has reminded me of my first time at sea and my first bout with sea sickness.

We were pulling out of port and probably were around one hour into going to sea when the nausea hit me like a ton of bricks. All I remember is leaning over the side of the ship and throwing up like crazy. And then I heard a bit of laughter as my Senior Chief came up to me and stated, "we are not even out of green water yet, you are gonna have a hell of a deployment shipmate!" Any sailors reading this book understand the term "green water" .... if you know you know.

During this time of sea sickness, I can honestly say I had never eaten so many crackers in my life! You see, when you have sea sickness, crackers are about the only thing you can eat without throwing it back up as soon as it goes down. Sea sickness sucks because there really is nothing you can do about it. You are at sea, the ship is continuously rocking back and forth, and *you cannot leave!* I still get nauseated just thinking about it to this day. If you ever experienced motion sickness you know what I am talking about. But, as it is with many things in life, you eventually get over it and in this case, once I was able to get used to it, going to sea was not so bad anymore.

After those short deployments we then received our orders to go to the Persian Gulf with the USS Eisenhower (the "Ike") Battle Group in support of Desert Storm and Shield. We departed Charleston, South Carolina for our forward deployment to the Persian Gulf that would last six months from what I recollect.

I have to be honest, I do not remember a lot from that deployment as it was so many years ago. But there are some particular memories that have stuck with me. One of them (and I am sure many sailors can attest to this), are the memories of being at sea and the calmness that surrounds you. As a deck seaman one of the watch-standing duties I needed to stand was the fore and aft lookout. The job of standing lookout watch was to "lookout" for contacts (ships) and report any findings to the bridge. For the aft lookout I would sit on the fantail of the ship with binoculars and the sound-powered phone. The fantail is the rear (stern) upper deck of the ship.

I remember many a night sitting out there in complete silence with nothing around but the ocean. Sometimes a beautiful moon rise would occur. Nothing is more beautiful than seeing a full moon come up from the horizon, it is awe-inspiring! Not to mention the serenity of hearing the water brushing against the sides of the ship, it was all just so calming, almost zen-like.

Then there was the Persian Gulf itself. There were times that the water was absolutely calm…, no waves, no ripples. It would literally look like a sheet of glass! You cannot really describe it, you just have to see it for yourself to really understand the serenity of it. Mother Nature can be very calming at times, and it definitely puts you in a place of peace.

Then, on the complete opposite end of the scale, there would be times that Mother Nature was having a bad day and we would be navigating through heavy seas. The waves would be so large and forceful that the fore and aft watches would be secured because it was too dangerous to be outside due to the waves crashing onto the ship. Yes, it is true as you sometimes see in pictures that the waves can get so high that they reach the Bridge. The Bridge is where the navigation team is located and the helmsman steers the ship. Being onboard a Fast Frigate in heavy seas is definitely not for the faint of heart! Keep in mind, the smaller the ship, the more it rocks and rolls in heavy seas and a Fast Frigate is a smaller ship! Imagine a cork in a bathtub. When you make some waves in the bathtub, that cork really gets to rocking and rolling.., this is a Frigate in heavy seas!

This reminds me of another funny story…

We were underway and I was the helmsman (I was steering the ship). Actually, this is a good point to make as many are surprised when they hear it. On a US Naval Ship the person who actually steers the ship is a young Deck Seaman, average age around 19 years old. Yes it is fact that the helmsman takes their orders from the Officer of the Deck (OOD), but the helmsman is actually the one who steers the ship and keeps it on course. You read that right, a young 19-something year old is the one whom steers a multi-million dollar US Naval Ship!

On this particular evening we were navigating some very heavy seas. I remember struggling to keep the ship on course and the Officer of the Deck constantly yelling "helmsman mind your helm!" This went on for a period of time as we navigated through the storm and heavy seas. Then (and I am not sure how it specifically happened) I accidentally steered the ship into a major swell and the ship rolled hard to starboard.

On the bridge there is an instrument that constantly measures the roll angle of a ship. It basically shows how far the ship is "leaning" to one side or another. Well, when I turned into that swell, I broke a new ships record for steepest "angle". All I remember is the Officer of the Deck shouting once again "helmsman mind your helm!" I heard the crashing of plates and dishes and everything down on the mess decks (cafeteria) went flying! Then the Commanding Officer aka "The Skipper" came flying up from his stateroom saying something like "what the hell is happening OOD!"

After everything was explained, the Skipper did not seem too bothered and actually had a bit of a laugh. He even made an announcement on the 1MC (the ships internal intercom) about how "Seaman Niznick steered us into a swell, you can thank him later" ..., or something like that.

I really cannot explain it, but it was crazy. All I remember is the ship started to lean, and lean and lean some more..., and I leaned against the lean with my body to maintain my balance. It honestly felt like we were going to capsize..., and I honestly thought I was going to crap my pants! I do not remember the angle we achieved, but it was one hell of a lean.

Another fond memory I have from those days aboard the USS Elrod is one of the collateral duties that I held. A collateral duty is a job or additional duty one has that is outside their normal day-to-day job. Collateral duties are in place to augment ships staff and help to spread some of the work load across the crew. My collateral duty was chocks and chains for the helicopters when they would land on the fantail of the ship. What this meant was, I was the one who would tie-down the helicopter once it touched down on the landing pad.

This was pretty frigging dangerous as is any job on the flight deck of a ship. The helicopter would come in, touchdown and the rotors would still be spinning. I would then run in (stooped over as to not get decapitated by the spinning rotors) and tie-down the helicopter using chains. There were pad eyes on the deck of the ship that were the anchor points used to tie-down the helicopter. It was enough to make your butt cheeks pucker a bit, but it was also helluva cool!

I always enjoyed my time on the flight deck. Every time they called "flight quarters, flight quarters" I would get a little giddy in anticipation of doing the tie-down of the helicopter. Plus it was a nice little break from the day-to-day duties of being a Deck Seaman underway.

But not everything was rainbows and unicorns serving aboard the USS Elrod. The next chapter speaks to an event that had happened to me while aboard the USS Elrod that is still in my mind to this day. It was also my first experience with a poor leader.

Ch.3: The Cheeseburger Incident

"Mess cranking". Anyone who has served in the US Navy knows this term all too well. For those who are unfamiliar I will do my best to briefly explain.

In the Navy when you go to your first command and are of the lower ranks (I was an E-2) you have to do a certain number of days mess-cranking. What this entails is you augment the ships cooking staff on the "mess decks" aka, cafeteria. Now although the majority of those who mess-crank support the main mess decks for all the enlisted (ranks E-1 to E-6), a few are chosen to work in the Chief's Mess (E-7 to E-9 eating area) or the Wardroom (Officers eating area). I was one of the "lucky" ones to be chosen for the Wardroom.

You have to understand that back in the day (not sure how it is now), the Wardroom was the only cafeteria to get real ice cream whereas everyone else received soft serve. Also, the Officers had the choice of selecting their breakfast, i.e., ham and cheese omelet, over easy eggs, etc... The same would go for lunch when "Sliders" were served. Sliders is a name we give to hamburgers in the US Navy. It is not known of the original roots of the term but it is said that way back in the day, sailors would call hamburgers sliders because they are so greasy they would just "slide" down a sailors gut...hence the term "sliders". An advantage of mess-cranking in the wardroom was I was able to partake in some real ice cream and also the cook I supported told me to cook up whatever eggs I wanted each morning for myself.., I must admit it was a pretty cool gig! And luckily, thanks to my mom, I actually knew how to cook so it was easy-peasy for me to whip some omelettes or over easy eggs for myself.

In addition to serving the Officers their food, I was also responsible to collect their dirty laundry, return their clean laundry and clean each stateroom. The stateroom is the Officers private room (quarters). Unlike Enlisted, Officers each have their own room with a small desk, bed, and ample storage space for their belongings. I will admit, doing this type of service work was challenging for me at first. I joined the Navy to learn a trade and be a Seabee and here I was collecting dirty skivvies (Navy term for underwear) and cleaning staterooms, it was a tough pill to swallow.

But, it was part of my duty so I did it to the best of my ability. Yes, I had to swallow some pride and humble myself, but doing this kind of service work at a young age did allow me to set some foundational leadership skills that I have retained to this day. It is a very humbling experience to be told you are now going to be a "steward" for the crew of Officers. But this experience allowed me to develop some customer service skills that have been a tremendous asset to me as I have navigated my career post-military. It was also one of those experiences that once again re-iterated what it means to be in service to others. The job itself was not particularly glamorous, but having that sense of service instilled into me early in my military career was something I am forever grateful for.

Being a steward of sorts, one of the things I was taught was how to serve the Officers their food. I was taught things like serve on the diners left, remove from the right..., it was like I was a waiter in a fine dining establishment! For the most part I was treated well by the Officers, though there was this one Lieutenant (O-3), a pilot, who was pretty arrogant. I remember when his glass would become half empty, he would just raise it with his right hand and hold it up until he garnered my attention, never saying a word. That was my cue to retrieve said glass and refill it for him. I still remember to this day how that would bother me immensely, especially given the fact that he would never say as much as a please or thank you. But in the military you have discipline, and I knew at the time it was my duty to serve the Officers in the Wardroom and I did it to the best of my ability.

During one lunch however, things just got plain out of hand. It was a sliders day. The Officers would check if they wanted a hamburger or a cheeseburger on the menu and what toppings they wanted. I would collect the orders and give them to the Mess Specialist (now known as a Culinary Arts Specialist) to make ready. Well, I did not keep track of everyone's orders, i.e., who ordered hamburger and who ordered cheeseburger, I just turned them in through the pass to the cook and he would let me know when the order was up. The cook brought up a plate to the pass for this particular Lieutenant and I served it to him. Well in just a few short minutes the Lieutenant waved me over with a look of disgust.

Now, this is where it gets *"good"*...

The Lieutenant said to me "Seaman Niznick, hold out your hand". I did as he had asked and he proceeded to *slowly peel* the cheese off the hamburger, *slap* the cheese in my hand, and then tell me "I wanted a hamburger *not a cheeseburger*". The image is still in my mind, clear as day, of when he put that cheese in my hand. I was shaking profusely because I was so frigging *pissed* off. I could feel my face getting red and I knew that the vein on my forehead had to be sticking out like a sore thumb. You see, I have this vein that tends to bulge out on my forehead when I am extremely upset or aggravated, I cannot hide it. It is kind of funny when I think about it because those who work on my teams (even to this day) know that when that vein starts bulging, I am extremely aggravated!

And on this day, at this moment, I am not going to lie.., I was pissed! It took *every* ounce of me not to haul off and deck him in the face right then and there. But I had military bearing and discipline. I knew he was an Officer and I was very junior Enlisted so I needed to respect the rank (not necessarily the person) which is an *important distinction.*

I went back to the pass and told the cook what had happened. Well, I do not know what kind of look I had (perhaps the bulging vein on my forehead was a dead giveaway), but the cook looked at me and said, "I don't know what happened out there but you look like you are going to snap, get out of here and take a break". And so, I did.

I do not think I need to say how fuming mad I was. I was *humiliated, degraded,* and *disrespected.* But through this poor leadership incident I did get to witness firsthand how a Chief in the Navy will *always* take care of their sailors. Later on that afternoon, the Senior Chief Mess Specialist came down and asked me what the hell had happened. As soon as I told him I could see the *anger* and *disgust* in his face. He said he would handle it and walked off. About an hour later he told me to go back to the Wardroom because the Lieutenant had something to tell me. I was reluctant but I did what Senior Chief had asked because I *respected* him.

When I arrived in the Wardroom it was just me and the Lieutenant. Let me tell you, you could cut the tension in the air with a knife! The Lieutenant approached me, somewhat hesitantly, and attempted to make an apology in the most *insincere* and *dishonest* way, but he made an effort nonetheless. Honestly, it would have been better if he had not apologized at all because of his insincerity. But I "kindly" accepted the apology and went about my day.

Only a choice few have ever heard this story until now. So, what made me write about this? Because it still *affects* me to this day and there is a *valuable* lesson to be taught. I will admit, it took years, *and I mean years*, for me to start respecting Officers again during my military career. I am ashamed to admit that I was very hateful to Officers after this incident and never spoke very highly of them for quite some time during my early Naval Career. But I did eventually realize that not all Officers were like this Lieutenant and as I progressed in my military career, I grew to respect them and actually have become friends with a great number of them. Heck, I even have mentored Officers during their military transition back to civilian life! It is amazing how things that go around, come around.

But even to this day I will admit that whenever I come across a person in leadership, I am very critical of how they speak and act, perhaps more than most. I believe this is due to how I was treated by a so-called "leader" back in my younger days when I was still very impressionable. Is my critical judgement unfair to those in leadership positions? Perhaps. But it only goes to show that how you *act* as a leader will make a *lasting* impression on those you lead for decades.... *do not ever forget that!*

As for me, I have held numerous leadership positions throughout my career and still do to this day. I will never forget the ole' Cheeseburger incident, it taught me a lot about how *not* to lead. I also pray that the Lieutenant found his way and came to realize that everyone is important in this world. No one is better than anyone else *regardless* of their chosen profession or education level..., we all bleed red.

Ch.4: Transfer To The US Navy Seabees

While still serving aboard the USS Elrod and deployed

to the Persian Gulf, my orders came in to go to Utilitiesman A-school. This was a story in itself. At the time I had the Senior Chief of the Command (a Boatswains Mate) really wanting me to stay in Deck Division. I also had another Senior Chief (a Quartermaster) whom took a liking to me as well and wanted me to strike Quartermaster. Quartermasters in the Navy are essentially the ships GPS. They navigate the ships course and they learn oceanography. It always seemed to be a cool job and I did take an interest in it while serving aboard the Elrod.

Striking into a rating means that you take the test for Petty Officer Third Class (E-4) for the rating that you want to become. If you pass the test and are advanced to E-4, you become that rating for your career. This process of striking into a rate bypasses the traditional process of attending A-School and receiving formal rate training as the majority of sailors do when they join the Navy.

I was actually starting to seriously think about striking to be a Quartermaster. I remember this Senior Chief teaching me basic celestial navigation while we were at sea.., that was really cool. I always had an interest in Astronomy and seeing this "old school" way of navigating by the stars was a really awesome experience! But after some serious self-reflection and speaking with fellow sailors, I ultimately decided to keep my A-school orders and report for duty to Gulfport, Mississippi.

I had to keep top of mind that I already had a guaranteed A-school and if I was to give that up and subsequently not pass or be promoted to Quartermaster Third Class Petty Officer, well, I would then be "stuck" in deck division. Not necessarily a bad thing, but when you have a guaranteed trade school, it would be silly not to attend it.

When the orders came in for my A-School, it proved to be "interesting" timing and made it a bit of a logistical challenge getting me off the ship and onto some flights to get me to my next duty station which was Gulfport, Mississippi. Our support of Desert Shield had ended and we were beginning our transit back to our homeport of Charleston, South Carolina. The Skipper (Commanding Officer) came up on the 1MC (ships intercom) and stated that we had an opportunity to cross the equator during our transit back.

Crossing the equator is a maritime tradition and also a US Navy tradition. For sailors whom this is their first time crossing the equator, there is a Shellback Initiation. This initiation is a traditional ceremony consisting of all kinds of shenanigans (at least back in my day, I understand nowadays it has been toned down a lot). Upon completion of the Shellback Initiation, one receives a coveted certificate to memorialize that experience. I am sure you can imagine my dismay when I heard this news about crossing the equator knowing I had to depart the ship, it really sucked! Being able to earn my Shellback would have been one of those awesome life experiences

I could have talked about to my kids and grandkids as I grew old. Oh well, I had to get off that ship and off to my A-School so I could become a US Navy Seabee!

So, let's go back to the logistical challenges of getting me off the USS Elrod. The Navy had to bring in a military helicopter to the ship so I could be picked up, flown off and taken to Bahrain. From Bahrain I boarded another aircraft that flew me back to the United States. I do not recall the flight itinerary specifically, but I do remember a lot of layovers and just seemingly flying all over God's creation.

It was around early 1992 when I reported to my A-School in Gulfport, Mississippi to begin my trade school/Seabee-specific training. A-School was a fun time and made for some interesting conversations for those of us who came through the targeted A-school program. For starters, we had many more ribbons on our uniform then the usual boot camp graduates. The instructors were surprised by this and did not understand how we had more ribbons than what they were used to seeing.

One must remember that the majority of A-School students have just graduated Boot Camp so they are still young and not very "seasoned" yet. You could see or at least sense the A-School instructors sense of surprise when we reported to class with a full row or maybe two rows of ribbons. Needless to say, they always made those of us with fleet experience the student leaders for the class.

A-School was a great technical instructional period that was thirteen weeks in duration for the Utilitiesman rating. We were taught the fundamentals of plumbing, heating, air-conditioning and refrigeration, pumps and compressors, and basic electrical theory. One thing to note about any military school is that they are fast-paced and cover a ton of ground in a short period of time. You really have to keep up and do a lot of after class studying to ensure you not only learn but retain the information that is put out.

The last course of instruction for the Utilitiesman A-school when I went through was boilers. I mention this because at the end of that course of training, we had to light off a boiler applying the steps that we were taught..., in proper order. There is a bit of science (or maybe physics is more accurate) involved with lighting off a boiler and the steps must be followed in exact order or the operator can incur serious damage to the boiler.

Please remember, the school was located in Mississippi back when I attended (it has since been relocated to Wichita Falls, Texas as a joint-service school with the Air Force). So, in true Cajun fashion, once boilers were lit off and we finished the final test, we would use the hot water to do a celebratory crawfish (mudbug) boil! Mind you, I am from Ohio, eating crawfish was not something I ever experienced before. But I am and always will be a foodie so I loved the opportunity to try this new food. Much to my surprise, I loved them. Heck, I even sucked the heads..., if you know you know! The crawfish boil was the perfect way to end the 13-week trade school before the formal graduation ceremony.

Upon graduation from A-School (and taking a 2-week leave period), I reported to my first Seabee Command, Naval Construction Battalion Seventy-Four (NMCB-74). The Construction Battalion was already deployed to Roosevelt Roads, Puerto Rico so I joined them on deployment. What an awesome first deployment with the Seabees..., Puerto Rico, how could anyone complain?!

Since I joined the Battalion late in their deployment, I was assigned to Camp Maintenance. Camp Maintenance is responsible for the maintenance and upkeep of the Seabee Camp. One thing I particularly remember about this deployment site was that our barracks were about 200 feet from the ocean. You could literally walk out of your barracks room with snorkeling gear and go snorkeling! And the water was absolutely gorgeous, the deepest and clearest blue I ever saw!

A US Navy Seabee Camp on deployment is liken to a small village or town. The camp consists of multiple buildings that support the Seabee Battalion Operations. A Camp consists of administrative buildings, medical and dental buildings, transportation building (where all the construction equipment is maintained), galley (cafeteria), Chapel, supply warehouse, and several other buildings to include the barracks where everyone sleeps and lives. As you can see, it really is like a small town or village. Camp Maintenance can then be referred to as a small Public Works. We have the responsibility to service and maintain all these facilities to ensure they are kept in proper condition to support the Seabees that inhabit them. Just as a local Public Works maintains and services the public facilities that support the town and its operations.

And now, for your reading pleasure, a junior plumber story...

While on deployment to Roosevelt Roads, Puerto Rico with Camp Maintenance one of my jobs as a Utilitiesman was to clean out the sewers that were throughout the camp. I was a young and green (slang for apprentice) Seabee and of course, being young and green you get all the not so glamorous maintenance jobs.

I will never forget the feeling of uneasiness as I stood over the manhole cover for the first time. The Second Class Petty Officer said to me something like "now UT3, when you go down there, do not look up and do not open your mouth". Well as it goes, when you tell someone who is "young" to not do something, what do they do?..., you guessed it, they do exactly what you told them not to do!

I climbed down the small vertical access ladder into this dark, moist, humid and hot manhole. I immediately heard this weird cracking type sound and of course looked up (thank goodness I did not open my mouth). Thousands, and I mean *thousands* of cockroaches were scurrying all above my head. And these were not your average size cockroaches either, they were frigging massive!!! And as I moved around and disturbed their environment, they scurried hastily with many falling on me! This is where the "do not open your mouth" comes into play. With these darn nasty cockroaches falling on me, I could only imagine if I had my mouth open...lunch anyone?

All I could think of at the time was "is this the adventure the Navy recruiters always talk about?" Any apprentice plumber who may be reading this book I am sure can relate. What a nasty job, but someone has to do it. Hell, I could of made it onto an episode of Mike Rowe's Dirty Jobs! I guarantee you, this was one job that we were not trained on or told about during A-school.

After that first deployment, I made two more deployments with NMCB 74 and they were back-to-back deployments to Okinawa, Japan. I do not know what it is about Okinawa but I found myself deploying there a total of four times in my Seabee career! Okinawa is just one of those deployment sites that is great to experience once, but anything more than that and it loses its luster. I mean honestly, there is only so much yakisoba one can eat!

It was during one of those Okinawa deployments that

I was selected to go through Jungle Warfare Training (JWTC) with the US Marines. The Seabee Battalions that deploy to Okinawa always look to send a few of their Seabees through this rigorous training. From what I recall, this is a one or two week long intense training course in the triple canopy jungles of Okinawa, Japan. Typically, the Marines would bring their basic bivouac gear and would eat MRE's (Meals Ready to Eat) for duration of the training. But we are Seabees and we do things a bit differently.

When we arrived, we set up proper tents and a galley (cafeteria). We actually brought the Navy cooks with us so they could keep in practice with field messing (cooking in the field environment) and we could have at least two hot meals per day, breakfast and dinner! Oh man, if you could see the looks on the faces of the young Marines that were across the way from us at their bivouac site..., *priceless!!* Here they were, sleeping in shelter-half's, eating MRE's for all three meals, every day and we, the Seabees, were living and eating "high on the hog" with fresh breakfast and dinner served daily.., those young Marines were definitely envious and probably thinking they joined the wrong branch of the military!

Jungle Warfare Training was no joke though, even with the two hot meals per day to keep us motivated. It is intense and physically grueling as anyone who has gone through it can attest. But the biggest challenge comes at the end of the training.

There is an endurance course that consists of different types of obstacles to negotiate. Two-rope bridge crossings, three-rope bridge crossings, rappelling, wading through muddy rivers, and all sorts of other challenges that we had to overcome as a team.

The last event of the endurance course is a formation run for about a half mile. But to make it even more challenging (despite the fact you are already completely exhausted) is throughout the endurance course you have simulated injuries. Some of the simulated injuries require you to place the injured Seabee onto a litter (stretcher). For the duration of the endurance course, a group of two or four Seabees have to carry the injured Seabee in the litter. So when it comes time to do that last run whilst carrying the litter, it is just physically and mentally demanding.

Needless to say, once everyone completes the endurance course, they are covered in mud, water and sweat. The instructors literally hose everyone down with a fire hose because it is the only way to get everyone cleaned up and honestly, it was one of the best feelings! You are literally covered in mud from head to toe and it is humid as hell, the firehose wash down is the best thing since sliced bread. Jungle Warfare Training Center, Okinawa, Japan is an awesome training exercise that I will always remember fondly.

Then there was the homeport training period and range

qualifications. Probably one of the most loved events for Seabees is going to the range and firing off some rounds. Due to my qualifying expert, I was chosen to be a range coach for one of our homeport periods. This was yet another collateral duty I had in addition to my primary job as a Utilitiesman. I loved being a range coach. There is nothing better then seeing someone on day one at the range, nervous and not shooting well (not even hitting the target in some cases) through your coaching and patience shoot to qualify.

I would work with them, hours upon hours, coaching them on trigger control, breathing techniques, and all the other skills one needs to qualify on a weapon at the range. And before they knew it, they would be firing off rounds, hitting the target, and eventually would receive a qualifying score. The look of determination and subsequent satisfaction and joy when they would finally obtain a qualifying score was priceless! Heck, some would even obtain sharpshooter, all the better!! But it was definitely a test in patience as a range coach. When people are nervous with firearms, they tend to do things that are not so safe. I remember plenty of time correcting them on muzzle control! That would be enough to make the butt cheeks pucker, let me tell you. But again, being a coach and watching someone go from not qualifying to qualifying, that was something that I will always remain proud of.

I transferred from the Battalion in 1995 and went on to

serve overseas for three years (1995 to 1998). Two years I was in London, England and one year I was in Souda Bay, Crete.

My tour in London, England is worth mention because that was my first exposure to data centers. I have actually found myself back in data centers as a civilian..., amazing how things always come full circle!

***

Before I reported for duty in London, England I had to attend C-1 Advanced school. C-1 Advanced school is advanced technical training in a particular skill or trade. C-school builds on what is taught at A-school and normally, once you graduate C-school you tend to have all future tours of duty leverage the specialized training you received. For me, the specialized training was Heating, Ventilation, Air-Conditioning and Refrigeration. The C-school was taught by the Air Force and was about 6 months in duration from what I recall. Upon completing my C-school, I was assigned as the sole HVAC technician for a US Navy Command in London, England.

This tour of duty was unique in that, it was civilian clothes duty. What this meant was, I did not wear my military uniform for the entire two year tour of duty. I was issued dark blue Dickies and this was my uniform for the next two years I was in London. The reasoning behind the civilian clothes duty was so we could remain "incognito" to the local British population. The intent was to not have anyone know the buildings we worked at housed US Navy personnel.

But, as I quickly found out, the locals were not fooled! I will never forget my first taxi ride from the airport. The cabbie asked where I was headed and I stated "7 North Audley". He immediately looked back and said "oh yeah, the US Navy building"! So much for being incognito. This command/building was decommissioned in 2007 and I recently discovered that as of 2022 it has been repurposed into luxury flats (apartments).

But I want to return to how this tour of duty was my introduction into data centers. I was the sole critical HVAC technician and was on call 24-7-365 for any cooling issues at the main building in London. This building contained a couple of floors of communications centers (data centers). We had a local maintenance team made up of military and local civilians that maintained the building. For the military team it was myself (HVAC technician), a UPS (Uninterruptible Power Supply) technician and a generator technician. Anyone who may be reading this and works in data centers can see that these three roles are exactly what is needed to maintain the critical facility infrastructure and ensure uptime of a data center in any environment or application. So, as I stated earlier, this was my introduction into data centers (I just did not realize it at the time). Luckily, during my two year tour, we never had a major engineering casualty and never brought down the communications center. We had some close calls with loss of critical cooling, but we were always able to restore cooling before equipment would overheat.

I am forever grateful for this tour of duty because it did lay the foundation of working in critical environments for me and it has proven to be an invaluable experience that I still lean on to this day. Thank God for being a Seabee!

My tour of duty in Souda Bay, Crete was only for one year so it was relatively short-lived. Be it as it may, it was another interesting tour where I did a job that was outside my normal rating of Utilitiesman. When I reported to Souda Bay I was told I would be working with two local Greeks moving furniture! Mind you, with my strong Air-Conditioning background I figured I would be assigned the HVAC/R maintenance shop but no, that was not what had happened. I was a little upset at the beginning because I loved being an HVAC/R service engineer and now I was being told I was going to basically be a mover.

In Souda Bay since it is only a one year tour of duty, Navy personnel are not authorized to bring any household goods (furniture, cookware, etc.). All of this is supplied to the servicemember when they rent their apartments on the local economy (if needed). Sometimes servicemembers would rent fully furnished apartments so they did not need anything from the Navy. But many did and that was my job along with my Greek local counterpart. We would deliver couches, recliners, love seats, coffee table, bed, mattress, the list goes on.

As each servicemember reported aboard Souda Bay, Crete they would come over to our household goods warehouse and let us know what they needed for their apartment. It was labor intensive work (as anyone who has worked for a moving company can attest). However, I did enjoy it once I got into the groove of the job. And my Greek partner in crime was an absolute joy to work with! He taught me quite a bit about Greek heritage and traditions during those many trips we took in the truck delivering and picking up household goods from the various apartments around the villages.

Honestly, this is a tour of duty I never given a lot of thought too until now. Looking back, I have some pretty great memories from my short time on the island of Crete. I had this island beater, a Ford Escort that got me around the island. It had some issues but was a good car to just get from point a to point b. It was also manual so it was a fun little car to drive around on the island! I also had my fair share of Greek Frappe's thanks to my Greek partner in crime who always made it a point to stop along our delivery routes to get some Frappe. Let me tell you, there is nothing like an authentic Greek Frappe, they are delicious!! And of course since Crete is an island, everyone knew my friend and partner in crime.

At first I would get annoyed with all the stops along our routes that he would make and just shoot the shit with his friends for what seemed like hours. But after awhile, I just sat back and enjoyed it, it was nice seeing the sense of strong community among the villages. They would speak in Greek so I never knew what they spoke about but I could see that my partner in crime was well known throughout the island. He had a lot of friends, let me tell you! But it was all in good spirit and we always got the job done and returned back to the base before knock off time.

Finally, this was yet another one of those tours of duty where I found myself in service to others. It was pretty cool delivering furniture and other household goods items to fellow Seabees and Sailors so they could have a nice place to live for their short one-year tour. And the furniture was actually pretty nice!

I mentioned earlier, we had recliners. That was something that I pushed for with my chain of command and they finally decided to fund the purchase. However, we only had a limited quantity so I had to manage the inventory closely. In true Seabee spirit, you can imagine who took priority in getting a recliner.... yep, you guessed it, my fellow Seabees!

Living and serving overseas for those two tours of duty were awesome. I was exposed to and learned a ton about the British and Greek cultures, way of life, and their respective history. I met some great local friends in each country and just enjoyed being a part of their world for a little while. The experiences and stories that were shared at various pubs in London were priceless. And learning about different Greek traditions while living in Crete, it was really a cool and unique experience that I am extremely grateful for. Of course, I could have done without going to the central trash disposal area on the island of Crete on a weekly basis. You have to understand that they still burn their trash in Crete. So every week my Greek partner in crime and I would take the trash that we accumulated over to this "burn pit".

I will never forget the smells and sights of this place! And the gentleman who worked the controlled burning of trash was an elderly man who definitely did not look the most healthy. Then there were Geep (a cross between goat and sheep) all over, covered in smoke and ash, and eating whatever scraps they found in the trash piles. It was definitely something to see and experience, let me tell you! I still every once in awhile have that smell come back to me, it is not a very pleasant memory. But this experience allowed me to appreciate some of those little things we take for granted in the United States, namely, waste management.

If you ever have an opportunity to work or live overseas I highly recommend it. Living and working overseas affords you the opportunity to see things from a different perspective which allows you to embrace a more diverse thought process. And having diversity of thought will enable you to be a more understanding and empathetic leader, traits that continue to be highly valued in today's society.

Ch.5: Haitian and Cuban Migration Of 1994

I need to rewind the clock for this chapter, please bear with me as this is one of those deployments that has stuck with me to this day.

It was August 1994 and I was with Naval Mobile Construction Battalion Seventy-Four and we were deployed to Okinawa, Japan (yes, Okinawa..., *again!*) We soon received our operations order (OPORD) to deploy to Guantanamo Bay, Cuba to build tent cities for Haitian refugees. Our initial tasking was to build a tent city to house approximately 6,000 refugees. Since it was only to be 6,000 refugees we assumed it would be a short deployment. Well, you know the saying about "Ass-u-me". Needless to say, our short deployment escalated rather quickly. By the time it was all said and done, we had to build a large enough tent city to house over 50,000 Cuban and Haitian refugees that were being funneled through Guantanamo Bay and then sent onward to

Florida.

But first, let me take you back to when we first arrived in Cuba as it is comical and a great example of failure to communicate among branches of service. We landed on the island and in true military fashion, when we arrived the local Marines had no idea who we were and why we were there. We explained that we would be building tent cities for the refugees, but the Marines just did not understand. Finally, after a lot of back and forth conversation, we were directed to a deserted Marine camp named Camp Buckley. It was run down but still had many wooden huts still standing and it was in these huts that we would initially set up our camp.

In true Seabee "Can Do" spirit, we immediately got busy improving our wooden huts. The Construction Electricians saw that none of the ceiling fans or lights were working. They got down to work immediately..., troubleshooting and bringing them all back to life. In Cuba (as you can imagine), having some ceiling fans to move air around was a monumental relief to everyone sleeping in those huts!

The mission was originally called Operation Sea Signal but as the tasking grew, it was renamed to Joint Task Force (JTF) -160 and would eventually include the Marines, Army and Air Force as well. Our (Seabees) mission was to build temporary shower units and tents for the refugees. We worked on average 18 hours a day,

7 days a week to accomplish the tasking. However, as more refugees started to arrive, our tasking increased exponentially, and we had to start finding other areas on the base to build the tents.

Finding other areas to build tents was not an easy thing to do. I will never forget the base Commanding Officer and how he was dead set against any tents being built on the golf course! I am not a golfer but from what I know, the golf course on Guantanamo Bay is absolutely gorgeous. Unfortunately, the decision was finally made to start building tents on the golf course, against the Commanding Officer's better judgement I might add. He did make it a point to have orange construction fencing placed around the greens, but all other areas of the golf course were free game for constructing more tents.

The entire Joint Task Force was not the most organized mission. I will never forget when our own Battalion Commanding Officer flew in for a visit with us and to meet with the JTF-160 Commander. After his meeting with the JTF-160 Commander he immediately came over to where we all were mustered (gathered) on another part of the island. From what I recollect, this was what he said to us: Seabees, I just came from the most f'd up meeting, no one knows who is in charge of this mission, it is a mess.

All we could do was laugh because we knew it to be true, hell, we were living it everyday we were on the mission!

Our Commanding Officer was a bit old school so he definitely told it like he saw it. He was not one for political correctness and when he would address his Seabees he was always blunt and honest. I always appreciated that about this particular Commanding Officer. He ended his "pep talk" by telling us how great a job we were doing, to just keep focused, finish the mission and get back to the rest of the Battalion.

This was my first Humanitarian mission, and I learned a lot. Seeing so many refugees desperate to leave their homeland and find a new life in the United States was an eye-opening experience. There were interview stations set up to interview all refugees. This was so those with any criminal backgrounds or anything else that would deem the refugee as not eligible to go to the United States could be identified and returned back to their homeland. Needless to say, many who were told they had to go back would end up taking their own life. There were a lot of suicides during this humanitarian mission…, much more than any of us anticipated or planned for.

What started as only Haitians migrating soon turned into Cubans as well. This was why the tasking grew so exponentially, thousands more unforeseen refugees started arriving to Guantanamo Bay. And when you have thousands of refugees living in close quarters, you get some troublemakers in the mix.

I will never forget when hundreds of them decided to

break out of the camps and run amuck on the base. They went into the McDonald's, the Base Exchange, etc... Needless to say, the Marine Security Forces took to action immediately and did what Marines do. It did not take too long for them to coral everyone back into the refugee camps.., with a little help from tear gas.

One thing that surprised many of us was all the free stuff the refugees received on a daily basis. Yes, they received the standard essentials like clothes and basic hygeine supplies. However, they also were receiving cartons of cigarettes, very nice shoes (Nike if memory serves me correct), and some other rather nice stuff, all through corporate donations. I will admit, at the time it was frustrating for me (and many of my fellow Seabees) to see because I thought of all the homeless US citizens in our own country and how they were always neglected. But, here were are all these corporations donating tons of stuff to these refugees without batting an eye. It just seemed so unfair to me.

Then there was the media, oh the good ole' media. I will never forget one time as I was working at one of the camps a couple of reporters were shooting some footage. As they were doing their report I overheard them say something like "look at this place, it looks like a prison! There is all this barbed wire everywhere, this is not the way we should be treating these human beings." This is where sometimes the media falls into the "perception is reality" bias. Yes, I guess looking back in hindsight, I could see how the reporters would have drawn this kind of tainted picture, they were not privy to the whole story behind the triple-strand concertina wire and why it was needed, but I was livid! I was also in a very emotional state of mind because of the long days and little sleep, so I am sure that did not help the situation either.

But nonetheless I was aggravated when I heard this reporter. I kept thinking to myself about how the refugees were being given all sorts of stuff for free and this reporter was going on and on about the perceived inhabitable conditions. To put this into perspective, the "barbed wire" they were referring to was the triple-strand concertina wire that we had to install around the perimeter of each refugee camp. We had to do this as an after action from when those hundreds of refugees escaped the camps and ran amuck on the island as I spoke about earlier.

Speaking of the triple-strand concertina wire…, it was actually not enough to keep the refugees in their camp! Believe it or not, they actually found ways to crawl their way through the wire and still manage to get outside their camp, it was crazy to witness!! And most of the time they were just escaping to capture some animal to cook for food. You have to understand, they were receiving Meals Ready to Eat (MRE's) and rice, but from what I remember, that was about it. So, they wanted something better and more substantial and the way they would get it was by capturing animals and bringing them back to camp to cook. It was really something to see. I still do not know how the heck they shimmied their way through triple-strand concertina wire, that is not an easy feat!

At the time I was too young to really have a grasp on the deeper meaning of what we were doing there. I was a young Seabee and was just focused on plumbing in the showers and tents and getting the job done. But as I have grown older, I have definitely thought back on that mission, many times. Although there was a lot of frustration, what we did for those refugees was truly in service to our fellow man. Our building the tent cities and other administrative areas assisted all the other Government Agencies and other military branches to carry out their mission of interviewing and vetting the refugees in mass quantities, allowing many to enjoy the freedoms only the USA can offer.

I do not know what kind of success stories may be out there from some of those refugees who planted roots here in the USA and gone on to raise a family and have a successful career. I am sure there are many and knowing what I and countless others did during this mission to make that happen for them, that is truly something I will always be proud of.

Ch.6: Recruiting Scandal

Recruiting duty. Any veteran who has had the opportunity to complete a recruiting tour will have their own stories and experiences to talk about. For me, what started out as a challenging tour of duty turned into a direct attack on my ethics and morals as a person.

Recruiting was a tough tour of duty for me because at the time, I did not think of myself as a salesperson. So why did I choose a recruiting tour of duty in the first place you may ask. Well, I did not have a choice to be honest.

I was within my 9-month window to transfer from Souda Bay, Crete. When you get within this window you contact your Detailer. I will speak to the Detailing process in more detail in a later chapter.

I called my Detailer and asked, "what do you have for me?" He eloquently stated "recruiting, recruiting or recruiting". Because I was not interested in sales, I refused and told the Detailer I would call the following month. During the Detailing process, you have about 3 to 4 months to decide on your next Command (tour of duty). You do not have to make a decision upon your first call to your Detailer and in this case, I didn't.

I called back at the beginning of the next month and the Detailer once again said "recruiting, recruiting or recruiting". I could see where this was going. I attempted to bargain with my Detailer, asking over and over "is there anything else?". He chuckled a bit and said straight up... "you have high marks on your performance evaluations, you do not have any NJP's (Non-Judicial Punishment), and in all respects, you are qualified for recruiting duty. We are short on recruiters so we have been directed to place anyone who is eligible into recruiting, no other option." Being as stubborn as I was, I said I would call back next month. The Detailer basically said that it would be the same story next month.

Well, he was right. When I called back for that third month, it was recruiting, recruiting or recruiting. But this time, just to reiterate, he stated "or you can get out of the Navy". Well, I was not ready to separate from service, so I reluctantly made the decision to go recruiting.

I reported to Navy Recruiting Orientation Unit (NORU) in 1998, attending school in Pensacola, Florida. I do not remember the duration of school, but I do remember the training. It focused on sales and all the communication techniques involved with sales, objection handling, prospecting, cold-calling, etc... Upon graduation I reported to my Recruiting Station where I would be for the next 3 years.

I was admittedly an average recruiter, I was by no means blowing it out of the water. I made goal, but not consistently. And of course there were a few months that I exceeded goal. As many recruiters will attest, recruiting duty is thirty-six (1) month tours of duty. We say this because one month you are the hero (make or exceed goal) and the next you are a zero (missed goal). It is truly a rollercoaster of emotions and stress!

About seven or eight months into my recruiting tour of duty things took a turn for the worse. Some conversations started happening among the recruiters about home-school. As the chatter became more prevalent, there was a mandatory meeting for the entire zone called. I will never forget this day. We all traveled to a central location to hear our Zone Supervisor speak about the home-schooling "initiative".

The conversation started out well. He spoke about how the Navy was going to start accepting home school graduates. Up until now, home schooling was not recognized as formal education by the US Navy and this closed the doors to a lot of potential candidates. Our Zone Supervisor went on to say how this would help so many civilians who want to serve their country in the US Navy, it was a great opportunity for them! And it was a great opportunity, I am not denying that.

However, the conversation then turned to how we should manipulate paperwork to make a candidate appear to be home-schooled. This is when my spidey-senses kicked in, this just did not pass the smell test with me. The all-hands meeting adjourned and we all went back to our recruiting offices and got back to work.

Over the next few months I continued to either barely make goal or miss goal. I did not have consistent performance month-to-month and my Recruiter-In-Charge took notice. He then began the conversation around home school. He would tell me things like "just do it, this is an easy way to meet or exceed goal". I flat out refused. Again, the whole thing did not pass the smell test and I was not going to be associated with any of it.

When my Recruiter-In-Charge was unable to persuade me, the Zone Supervisor then got involved. He called me and basically said the same thing.... Just do it, it is easy to do and you can get so many more people in the Navy and give them this great opportunity! I held my ground and refused to play the game.

Then one day when I was at the Military Entrance Processing Station (MEPS), the First Class Petty Officer who led the Navy Office came to me and asked if I wanted to be a Classifier. This was completely out of the blue and unexpected. He and I befriended one another over the months while I was bringing candidates in to be processed and join the Navy. He always took notice of me and how I interacted with his staff. As a recruiter, you have the duty to drive to the MEPS any time you have candidates "on deck", meaning they plan to join the Navy that day.

One thing I learned early on in my recruiting tour was to make friends with everyone at the MEPS. As you can imagine, not everyone is always ready to sign a contract on processing day. If you are that candidates' recruiter, this is one of the most frustrating challenges you have to overcome. I had a few do this to me while I was a recruiter and I can attest, it is not fun to deal with!

I learned quickly however that if you make friends with the MEPS staff they will look out for you. When you do have a "shaky-Jake" who starts to get cold feet and refuses to sign, the MEPS staff will work with that individual and try to get them to overcome their own fears. But, they will only do this if that candidates recruiter is not a jerk! I saw many recruiters treat the MEPS staff terribly and I would shake my head. It was those same recruiters that when they got a candidate with cold feet, the MEPS staff would do nothing to assist, and I mean nothing.

So, for me, having those great relationships with the MEPS staff paid off. I took the First Class Petty Officer up on his offer to be a Navy Classifer.

Plus, looking back, I see how God had His hands in this as well. I was being pressured to do something very dishonest and I was refusing to do it. I *never* gave-in to the pressure or group-think that was happening. I truly believe that my staying true to my core values and morals was enough for God to turn things around for me and get me out of that environment and to the MEPS. Not to mention, I had to move to a new location closer to the MEPS and it was after that move that I met Sheri....my future wife! You cannot tell me God did not have His hands in this!!

Ch.7: Meeting "The One"

Beside God, there is absolutely no one who has influenced and guided my life so significantly as my wife Sheri. I cannot capture everything she has done for me in our time together as it is nearly impossible. But her impact on me is significant and worthy of its own chapter.

I was on recruiting duty and as I stated in the previous chapter, I needed to relocate for my new position as a Navy Classifier working from the Military Entrance Processing Station. As it goes with the Navy and relocating, I needed to find an apartment and find one fast! I came across an apartment complex and the rental representative showed me the single bedroom apartment that was available. I immediately signed the rental agreement and moved in.

This rental representative was a friend of Sheri. As the story is told to me by Sheri, this rental representative wrote Sheri a letter that she had met someone through the course of renting an apartment. Sheri at the time was in California with her sister. Upon reading the letter from her friend, Sheri immediately had some inner feelings and she looked at her sister and said something along the lines of "God is telling me this is the man I am supposed to marry". I cannot explain the details of these feelings because I am not Sheri. However, I do know that Sheri has exceptionally strong intuition and for her to have these thoughts is not really all that unusual. I am unsure how her sister took the news, but I am sure she thought that there was no way of knowing that at this point in time.

I will never forget when we first started dating. I knew

immediately that there was something different going on. I had very strong feelings for Sheri from day one. I had never experienced this before and I will be honest, it kind of scared me. Many speak about love at first sight and if it is really possible…, well I can say, it is possible and it happened with me!

At the time we started dating I was battling my own internal struggles. I really did not want to believe that I was "in love". I always said that I would not marry while serving in the military. I did not want to "burden" my spouse with the stress of military life. And although I "believed" this, something about Sheri kept drawing me in. Before we knew it, we were dating and connecting on a much deeper level.

I realized Sheri was "the one" for me as well and decided I would propose to her.

However, before I begin that story, I want to take a minute to go back to what I stated earlier about having my own internal struggles. At the time I was well on my way to becoming an alcoholic, drinking a case of beer just about every night. Throughout our dating Sheri observed my heavy drinking and was not impressed. Then one day she just turned, looked me dead in the eyes and said, "I will not be a part of this, you need to make a decision".

Wow, this was enough to make my brain go into a tailspin. I went into defensive mode. I was thinking "how the hell could this person say this to me"? After all, I was having a successful Naval Career, my life was going good and I did not see it as a problem, at least not at the time. But after some deep thought and reflection and after overcoming my initial defensiveness, I realized I loved Sheri, and I was going to put her first.

I am so glad I made that choice so many years ago because I would not be the person I am today without Sheri by my side every step of the way. Sheri has always been my number one supporter and she has always believed in me, even when I did not believe in myself.

But on a lighter note, let us go back to the story of how I "popped the question", I am sure you will find it entertaining.

While on recruiting duty, every year we would have a training and awards conference. I decided that I would propose to Sheri at the annual conference in 2000. I planned this proposal for months beforehand, ensuring a few of my civilian co-workers at the Military Entrance Processing Station were in on it…hey, one of them had to hold the ring during the conference! It went down picture perfect. The Executive Officer presented me with an award that I knew was coming, and then proceeded to call Sheri up to the stage. Sheri had no idea what was about to happen! In tradition, I went down on one knee and proposed to Sheri in front of about three hundred fellow Sailors…if you could hear all the yelling and cat-calling from the sailors, it was priceless! No one was expecting this proposal.., thankfully she said "yes" ...and the rest (as they say) is history!

This was probably one of the craziest proposals given. Having over three hundred sailors screaming, cheering, and hollering after she said "yes" is something I will never forget. Soon thereafter we set our wedding date, September 22nd, 2001. Little did we know at the time how that date would become very significant and emotional.

It was getting close to our wedding date and the usual stress of wedding planning was at an all-time high. Collecting RSVP's, finalizing details for the wedding and reception, etc... all those things a young couple goes over in finite detail to ensure everything is good to go. Then 9-11 happened and all this work and stress became insignificant.

I was still on recruiting duty when those events occurred. I will never forget that morning as we were in-processing candidates who were going to be joining the Navy that day. All of a sudden, we were glued to the television at the Military Entrance Processing Station (MEPS). All processing stopped and we just sat and watched the tragic events of that day unfold.

It is not my intent to reopen that dark part of our American history, everyone has their own memories of that day. But after a few days had passed, Sheri and I were facing a decision.., do we proceed with the wedding or cancel? We had family coming in from all over the United States and at the time air travel was still in disruption. We had no idea what the future held regarding travel safety and overall feelings everyone had about those tragic events.

Sheri and I discussed all options at length. Finally, Sheri looked at me and said, *"we need to have this wedding."* In her view it was what was needed for our family and friends to give them a chance to have some joy among all the sadness and despair that had happened to our country. I agreed and we kept the wedding as planned.

Looking back, I am so glad we kept it on the original date. Dare I say it was the best darn wedding and reception ever! I think it was everyone's little escape from all the evil that had happened, and it just gave everyone a chance to enjoy the moment. It was truly an incredibly special day.

And from that day, my life began down a new path. As I stated earlier, Sheri has driven me further than I would have ever gone on my own. She has always seen things in me that I did not see myself. Sheri has always believed in me and pushed me out of my comfort zone more times than I care to admit!

First, she brought me back to my faith and church. Let me say that my mom, even through all the trials and tribulations of divorce and being a single mom, never missed church on Sunday. So church was a part of my upbringing, no doubt about it. But when I joined the military, I have to admit, church fell by the wayside. I was too involved with other extracurricular activities and I just did not find church as a foundational part of my life. But Sheri changed that and I am forever grateful for it. God is now front and center in my life.

Then there is college. As I spoke to previously, there was no college in my immediate family. And for me, I was not the least bit interested in formal education. I had learned invaluable skills as a tradesperson, and I had every intention of gaining employment post-military in the trades. But Sheri was adamant that no matter what I decided to do post-military, I needed to obtain a degree. As she stated repeatedly, the Navy is paying for it, why not just do it?!

I will be honest, I was reluctant to begin college because

I was *scared*, plain and simple. I did not think I was "smart" enough to go to college. I was not the stellar student in public school, and I was never into academics. So, I made excuse after excuse to not apply to college. But Sheri is persistent, and she did not accept my excuses.

It took 8 years, yes that is right, *8 years* before I finally decided to apply to college. We were living in Annapolis, Maryland stationed at the US Naval Academy. I applied and was accepted to Anne Arundel Community College. I began to work toward my AAS, Introduction to Engineering. Unfortunately, we transferred out of Maryland and I was not able to complete all the courses for that degree. My college pursuit was put on hold.

But Sheri was not one to let up. She kept asking me when I was going to go back. And again, I started with the excuses...and again, she did not accept them. In 2010 I made the decision to apply to the University of Maryland University College (now known as the University of Maryland Global Campus) for my B.S., Environmental Management. I have always had a strong interest in the environment, in particular, water management. I really liked the curriculum of this degree and decided what the heck, what do I have to lose? Ironically, after 3 years of rigorous studies I graduated from UMGC the same day as my retirement from the US Navy Seabees, August 31st, 2013... that was one heck of a day!

Sheri has and always will be *my rock and my strength*.

She always provides me with honest counsel and lets me know directly when I am messing up, especially when it comes to my positions held in corporate America. She is the first to tell me when I say something stupid or when I am cussing a bit too much or just not presenting myself in the best of light.

When I first transitioned out of the military, I had a *big ego* on my shoulders. I talk about this in more detail in the chapter on military transition but it is worth mentioning here as well because it is so important.

I was arrogant and it showed, and Sheri was always quick to point it out to me. I did not always accept her counsel positively, after all, I was a Navy Chief! But what I failed to realize and what Sheri continued to impress upon me was the fact that I *was* a Navy Chief. No one out in corporate America really gives a hoot about what I did as a Navy Chief.

This was a hard pill for me to swallow. And honestly, if it were not for Sheri, I do not think I would have ever swallowed it! Sheri continued to provide wise counsel and told me things to the effect of until I get the ego knocked off my shoulders, I will not go far in the civilian world. Although I did not like hearing it, I knew it to be true. I eventually came around, it "only" took two or three years. Yes, I tend to be a bit stubborn!

I can go on and on about what Sheri has done for me and how she has made me a better person, man, husband

and father. But I will sum it up by saying that God brought us together for a reason. As it goes with any strong marriage, we make each other whole. I would *never* have achieved what I have achieved if it were not for Sheri and her *belief in me* over the years. She tells it like she sees it, she keeps me on the straight and narrow. I am *blessed* to have her as my beloved.

Ch.8: Making Chief Petty Officer

It is only fitting to follow the Chapter about Sheri to the Chapter of my earning the title of Chief Petty Officer. Again, it was Sheri who believed in me and never allowed me to not apply my full effort into anything when it came to my military service. She always supported my Seabee career and knew how badly I wanted to make Chief Petty Officer. So, when I would do stupid things that would possibly hinder my making Chief, she was the first one to call me out! That all came together when I received the call and was informed that I was selected for Chief Petty Officer in the US Navy Seabees.

Before I go into the day I found out I was selected for

Chief Petty Officer, it is a good time to talk about how advancement to Chief Petty Officer works in the US Navy. There are three phases to this particular advancement. First, one must take the E-7 (Chief Petty Officer) rating exam. Just as one does for all other advancements in the Navy, you have to take this rating exam and pass in order to be eligible for Chief. It is a multiple choice exam consisting of 150 questions from what l remember. It is also a timed exam, I think one has 2 hours to complete the exam. A few weeks after completion of the exam cycle, a list is distributed stating who made board.

Board refers to the selection board for Chief Petty Officer. If you make board, this means that your service record will be reviewed with scrutiny over a period of months by Master Chiefs and Senior Chiefs to determine if your performance and experience is enough to be selected for advancement to Chief Petty Officer. It is also at this time that the servicemember has the opportunity to review their service record and ensure there are no missing awards or anything else that would prove beneficial to being selected for advancement to Chief Petty Officer. If there are, they have the opportunity to send in this missing documentation to the board for their review.

The board process is very tightly controlled and is held in secrecy to avoid any outside influence from deterring the results. Finally, once the board convenes and they have made their selections, the list of Chief selects is communicated to all Commanding Officers.

***

Chief Petty Officer aka *"The Chief"*. This rank in the US Navy holds much prestige and is perhaps the single-most proudest achievement of any Enlisted Navy Sailor in their career. A Chief Petty Officer in the US Navy holds the highest amount of authority and responsibility within the senior enlisted ranks as compared to all the other military branches of service. With this great authority and responsibility comes an intense "training period" for six weeks prior to being officially advanced in rank to Chief, sometimes referred to as "Chiefs' Initiation". We (Chiefs) all have our own stories of how we obtained this rank and are proud of those Anchors we earned. For me, it was something that I honestly did not see coming!

It was my fourth time being eligible for Chief with the three previous times going unselected. I was not optimistic that I would make it this time around because for this cycle, the Navy Seabees were only advancing four Utilitiesman First Class Petty Officers to Chief. To put this into perspective, there were approximately one-hundred Utilitiesman eligible for Chief for this cycle.

I was at home with Sheri on the day the results were scheduled to be announced. I honestly did not feel my name would be on the list so I headed home after taking care of some morning business at the Battalion offices. But then the seemingly "impossible" happened....my cellphone rang, and it was from my Commanding Officer aka "The Skipper". As stated earlier, it is customary and tradition that the Commanding Officer of the Command is the first to let Chief Selects know of their selection to Chief Petty Officer.

I could not believe it, I was flabbergasted! I remember seeing Sheri out of my peripheral vision, she knew what that call was and the excitement she had for me was showing. He then handed the phone over to our Command Master Chief who also congratulated me but then (as any Chief would do) immediately ordered me to get my ass to the Battalion offices ASAP! The "games" began. As soon as I hung up the phone, I told Sheri I was selected for Chief. She embraced me with the biggest hug ever and of course many kisses! I told her I had to report to the Battalion offices and although visibly upset, she understood.

Anyone who knows anything about the US Navy and the selection process to Chief Petty Officer understands that this is a tremendous training evolution, or more accurately, an initiation. It involves approximately 6 weeks of intensive training that equates to long days and even longer nights. The reason for this is to transform the Chief Select from thinking as an individual contributor to thinking and acting as a leader. It is to get them to not put themselves first but rather, put their troops first. Just as it is for any civilian who moves into a leadership role, it takes a huge adjustment to change from thinking of oneself to thinking and putting others first. This is at its core the idea behind the initiation to Chief Petty Officer in the US Navy. After the initiation and when you are officially welcomed into the Chief's Mess, you become the technical leader, you become "The Chief".

As I stated earlier, I was one of four selected this cycle. Believe you me, the Genuine Chiefs (this is what we call all the active and retired Chief Petty Officers) especially the Utilitiesman Chiefs' let me know this time and time again throughout the Initiation season! "You are one of four, you are one of four"... you can only imagine how they worked that into every damn training session I had.

Chiefs Initiation is a time-honored tradition and one that is held in secrecy so I will not speak to the Initiation itself. I will also say that over the years, this tradition has been questioned by many in the Navy as to its validity and relevance in "todays Navy". It is a shame really, and even when I was serving, there was always a few that did not understand why we had a Chief Initiation. Some view it as hazing, nothing more, nothing less.

But for those of us who go through it, we know it to be so much more than that and we understand its significance. For me (and everyone else who has gone through this initiation) it tried, tested and challenged me beyond anything I ever experienced and that is exactly what it is meant to do! And there are many training evolutions that take place that at the time, you (the Chief select) may not fully understand its significance or the lesson/s that it is teaching you. But, as many Chiefs know, those lessons do become clear later on in your career as a Chief Petty Officer. They become those ah-ha moments that make you see clearly the lesson being taught at the time.

September 16th, 2004 is the day I was "pinned" to Chief. As all Chiefs like to say, it is a day I will never forget.

The ceremony itself is quite the military event. The ceremony is meticulously planned in strict military fashion and we have several practices prior to the actual ceremony itself. One of the special moments is that all the new Chiefs get to select who "pins" on their Anchors. The Anchors are the rank insignia that are worn on the shirt collars to indicate your rank in the military. Up to First Class Petty Officer, that rank insignia is a crow with chevrons below. But when you make Chief, that insignia changes to a Gold Fouled Anchor that represents stability and security. It also includes USN across the middle of the Anchor which stands for Unity , Service, Navigation.

The formal act of pinning on the Chief Anchors for the first time is a highly emotional experience for all involved. For my pinning, Sheri and my mom pinned on the Anchors with Sheri pinning one collar and my mom the other. I will not say too much more about this moment. If you want to know more, I suggest Googling "Navy Chief Pinning Ceremony", you will get more information and images than you know what to do with!

However, pinning day and being advanced to Chief Petty Officer is a professional achievement that I am proud to have earned. It took me thirteen years of service to get selected and accepted into the Chief's Mess and I would have not had it any other way. And to have Sheri by my side on that very special day, well, that was the icing on the cake!

Ch.9: 2004 Indian Ocean Tsunami

It was October of 2004 and immediately following my pinning ceremony that advanced me in rank to Chief Petty Officer, I was assigned as the Operations Chief for a detail of 50 Seabees. This assignment as Operations Chief would prove to be a great personal lesson on leadership and motivating troops, especially considering the fact I was a new Chief.

We were in homeport (garrison). What this means in military lingo is we were in the United States for our training and administration period. For the command I was assigned, Naval Mobile Construction Battalion (NMCB) 40, our homeport was Port Hueneme, California. I think it is also necessary to explain the deployment cycle when assigned to an NMCB. The typical rotation is 12 months in homeport and 7 months deployed.

As it happens sometimes when drawing near to deployment, the command will receive word of where they will be deploying. And quite honestly, when some hear of where that will be, many become quite emotional. For our detachment, we received word that we would be going to Iraq. Specifically, we were going to Camp Anaconda. Camp Anaconda was also known as Camp Mortarville because of the daily but highly *ineffective* mortar attacks that occurred.

Some of the Seabees on this detail became quite emotional. Some did not want to go to war, plain and simple. They joined the military for other reasons and did not foresee having to go to war. As crazy as that may seem, this is what happens sometimes when reality hits and service members realize that war is real, and they are now going to be a part of it.

As the Operations Chief, I was the one the Seabees would come to when they needed to vent or air their concerns. I remember a few that were downright scared to go to Iraq, I did not blame them. No one wants to go to war and quite frankly it is not something that excites anyone in the military. But we do have our duty to uphold and when duty calls, you must answer that call. As it were, it took time to deal with the initial emotions of the Seabees and get them to accept the fact that we were going into harm's way aka "going to war".

However, as these things sometimes go in the Navy Seabees, our orders to Iraq were going to be changed. I will never forget how our Commanding Officer at the time put it to us at an all hands call. He said something to the effect of "we are like the end of a wagging tail on a dog, our mission changes frequently and without any real rhyme or reason". And this is what had happened a few times and it was not fun. One day we were going to Iraq, the next day we were not. Then a week or two later were going to Iraq, a few days or weeks later, we were not.

Finally, it ended up being that we were going to deploy with the rest of the Battalion to the main deployment location which was Okinawa, Japan. As our Commanding Officer stated to our detachment, let's just get you all over to Okinawa and from there we will figure out what to do with you (or something along those lines). So much for military "strategy".

My team of Seabees were angry, or at least most of them were. We trained and we had everyone motivated and onboard with deploying in support of the Global War on Terrorism only to have that cloth ripped out from under our feet. It was infuriating but there was nothing we could do about it. So off we went, to Okinawa, Japan.

From what I remember we deployed around November of 2004. Soon thereafter, December 26th to be exact, we heard of a massive Tsunami that went through the Indian Ocean and completely devastated everything in its path. We immediately had a strong feeling that we would now be going there to assist with disaster recovery efforts.

The Navy Seabees are well known for our strong capabilities in disaster recovery and humanitarian missions. Due to our vast construction skills and having access to heavy construction equipment, it is a no-brainer that when major disasters strike, Seabees will be called to action. And this is exactly what happened. We were given our Operations Order to deploy to Banda Aceh, Indonesia to support the disaster recovery efforts.

A little-known fact about the Navy Seabees is we are trained to deploy within 72 hours (about 3 days) of any deployment order. So, as soon as we received the official word of our mission, we went immediately into embarkation mode. As Operations Chief, I was responsible for the hour-by-hour activities to ensure the troops were ready, CESE (Civil Engineering Support Equipment) was prepped for embarkation, reports were being drafted, and all other administrative and operational taskings needed to deploy our unit were completed. To move a unit of 50 Seabees is a coordinated effort among many stakeholders, both within the deploying unit and the support elements. And as you can imagine, it is a 24/7 operation.

We were assigned to the USS Bonhomme Richard LHD-6 who transported our Seabee detachment and CESE to the area of operations (AOR). We arrived into the area of operations on January 5th, 2005, but to our dismay we were not allowed to go to Banda Aceh, Indonesia at this time. There was some political pushback from the local Government of Indonesia. They were not going to allow any US military service members into their country to render help. I am not 100% sure why this was to be honest. I know there was talk that they feared we were going to spread Christianity and Western World ideals, but I am not sure if that was fact or fiction.

What I do know is my Seabees (and I) were frustrated. We were in the middle of the ocean, basically doing circles, awaiting any official communication that we could move forward with the mission. And for us (Seabees) our mission was to go inland and perform engineering assessments of government and educational facilities. As teams of 5-10 Seabees, we were to inspect the facilities for structural integrity and make our recommendations on whether the facility could be inhabited or not.

There is one thing to keep in mind when it comes to disaster recovery efforts. Everyone wants to get back to as much of a state of "normalcy" as possible and as quickly as possible. This was the basis for the structural assessments. Once we performed an assessment and deemed the facility habitable, the people who worked there could get on with their work to the best of their abilities given the environment they were in.

Finally, after from what I remember to be about one or two weeks later we received word that we could go into Banda Aceh and carry out the mission. But there was another unsuspected turn of events, *they did not want us to bring in our Construction Equipment!* This was frustrating because we wanted to also help clear roads to aid with relief efforts. But the local Government was persistent and denied our requests to bring some of our construction equipment (CESE) into Banda Aceh.

I remember one time when I was in Banda Aceh, a gentlemen came up to me and asked if we had a bulldozer. I told him we did but it was on the ship and we were ordered not to bring it ashore. He was livid, explaining that all the bulldozers they had were inoperable due to water damage and other damages incurred by the Tsunami. It was definitely a strange dilemma. I still to this day do not fully understand why the local Government leaders restricted what we could and could not do in support of the disaster relief efforts. We could have done so much more if we were allowed to bring in our heavy construction equipment.

But we did carry out the mission and completed it

without fail. We performed a total of fifty structural assessments of government and educational facilities. One cool responsibility I had was to debrief the Deputy Governor of Indonesia periodically on our progress and findings. Myself and our Assistant Officer in Charge (AOIC) whom was a Senior Chief Petty Officer would hold these briefings. We did a few of these briefs and they were very enlightening to all parties involved.

I want to go back to the engineering assessments because there was one in particular that weighs heavily on me to this day. I was by myself (not sure how that happened to be honest). I was told to get into a vehicle with a local where he would take me to a facility that needed a structural assessment performed.

I will never forget that car ride. We drove past so much devastation.., it is indescribable. I remember passing the mass graves...basically huge holes in the ground where hundreds of bodies would be placed and buried. They basically loaded the bodies into these holes and then covered everything back up with dirt. Because of the thousands of bodies (there was approximately 170,000 dead or missing in Banda Aceh), this was the quickest way to bury them and lay them in their final resting place.

We finally arrived at the location to be assessed after what was about 45 minutes of driving through small villages that were just annihilated. I was dropped off and told to head to a building straight ahead that the driver pointed out to me. I was then left on my own to perform the engineering assessment. To be honest what happened next is a bit of a blur, but this is what I remember to the best of my recollection.

I was in the middle of performing an engineering assessment on a school facility when a highly distraught mother with a baby approached me. Honestly, she startled me a bit as she seemingly came out of nowhere. I was not anticipating seeing anyone as I performed this assessment. She started asking if I had water as best she could considering she did not speak fluent english. I could see that her baby appeared lifeless, and this mom was in desperate need of help. The look of desperation in her face was one that I will never forget.

All I had was my canteen. I told her I had no water to give. She kept asking me but I insisted that I had no water to give. She finally (after what seemed an eternity) turned around and walked away. I was left an emotional wreck.

I constantly relive this situation in my head. I feel like I was being *selfish*.

What the hell was I thinking?

Do I have regrets? No. But do I wish I would have approached this situation differently... *hell yes*...If I could rewind the clock, I would have done things differently, that is for sure. I will never know what happened to that mother and child, but I think of them often.

***

One of the main things that added to the emotions of us Seabees during this humanitarian mission was the fact that the majority of the victims were women and children. This hit us especially hard. We were the only military unit that were going as far inland as we were. We saw much more death than we had anticipated and it was emotionally draining. This is something you cannot prepare for mentally. I told my Seabees before we deployed into the region that this was going to be different for them. Performing humanitarian missions is not like going to war, it takes a different mindset. They quickly realized what I had meant when they started seeing the deceased women and children that were everywhere.

Whole families were wiped out (for lack of better terms). I remember one time an older gentleman came up to me and in very broken English stated that he was the only person left in his entire family tree. It took me awhile to understand what he was trying to tell me, but once I did, I just could not believe it. His whole family tree was gone, deceased, and he was the sole survivor. Can you imagine that? How do you console someone after they tell you something like that? It was just crazy and emotionally draining.

I do not want to end this chapter on a low however.

One thing that was awesome to witness was the strength of the human spirit. Everyday that we went inland to perform our mission, we were met with smiles. Yes that is right, smiles! These people lost everything and had to rebuild their lives from scratch. But they still found reason to smile. That spoke loudly to me and has stuck with me to this day. Whenever I am having a bad day or work is getting stressful, I think back to those smiles among the death and devastation and just give myself a bit of a reality check. If they were able to find joy in all their despair, why can't I when faced with stress or just plain old corporate or life shenanigans? It was truly inspiring to see that human spirit among all the devastation.

After what I believe was about two or three months, we finished our humanitarian mission in Indonesia and returned to Okinawa, Japan to complete our Battalion deployment. I was assigned as the Camp Maintenance Chief for the remainder of that deployment.

As Camp Maintenance Chief, I had yet another leadership challenge that presented itself.

But before we move on to that story, I want to share some facts about the Tsunai that will put this mission into better perspective for all whom are reading this:

> 1. The waves that came ashore in Banda Aceh, Indonesia topped 100 feet.

2. The tsunami's waves traveled across the Indian Ocean at 500 Miles Per Hour.

3. The Indonesia earthquake caused a shift in the Earth's mass, changing the planets rotation.

4. Death toll in Banda Aceh, Indonesia was in excess of 100,000.

5. It was one of the deadliest natural disasters in recent history.

6. The earthquake that initiated the tsunami was measured between 9.1 and 9.3 magnitude and was the third largest earthquake since 1900.

Ch.10: Never Give Up On Those You Lead

I was a "new" Chief Petty Officer meaning I was recently advanced to Chief and this was my first deployment as "the Chief". Upon returning from a forward deployment to Banda Aceh, Indonesia, I was assigned as the Camp Maintenance Chief and was responsible for the direct supervision of about fifty maintenance and administrative personnel. We had a great team except for one Seabee.

This Seabee always found themselves in some sort of trouble. Whether it was off-duty incidents or missing morning muster (being late for work for the non-military types reading this), this Seabee was always finding themselves in bad situations. Being the Chief I was responsible for leading, coaching, developing and when necessary, disciplining my team members. Needless to say, I had this Seabee in my office numerous times for counseling. This Seabee just always found themselves in some sort of trouble, on and off duty.

In the Navy we have what we call the "Chief's Mess". This is the place where all the Chiefs' in the command get together to discuss command issues, troop issues, Commanding Officer's initiatives, etc... It is also where the new Chiefs' get some great mentoring from the more senior Chief Petty Officers in the Mess. As it is with the Chiefs' Mess, everyone knows when you have a problem Seabee. So, I was pulled aside by a Senior Chief whom I admired and respected. He said "Randy, you must know when to give up. Seabee "X" is more problems than they are worth, you are spending too much of your time on them. Send them to Captain's Mast and let the Commanding Officer hand out the appropriate disciplinary action".

This hit a nerve with me as I was not ready to "give up" or "throw in the towel" on this Seabee. I do not know what it was about this Seabee but something in my heart said I needed to continue to handle the situation at my level and not escalate it to a Captain's Mast. I could see this Seabee was hurting on the inside, although they played "tough guy" on the outside. There was just something about this Seabee that told me to not give up regardless of the numerous headaches they were giving me.

So, I didn't.

Between me and my Platoon Commander, we both continually counseled and watched over this Seabee for the duration of the deployment. It was not without some serious trials and tribulations that is for sure! However my Platoon Commander and I knew we could not give up on this Seabee, we just could not give up, no matter what.

Well as it is in the Navy, upon return from deployment my tour of duty was complete and I was transferred to another duty station, the US Naval Academy in Annapolis, Maryland. I gave my departure speech to my great maintenance team and transferred to Annapolis, leaving it all behind me…or so I thought.

About six years later, yes that is right., *six years* later I received a friend request on Facebook from the Seabee that gave my Platoon Commander and I so much trouble. Well, I accepted the request and thought nothing more of it. A few weeks went by and I received a message from this Seabee. They said that they had since separated from the Navy Seabees, Honorably, and were working in Corporate America.

Then the big news came out…

This Seabee went on to tell me how they got their life together and were enrolled in college for a degree!!!! This Seabee ended the message by thanking me and my Platoon Commander for never giving up on them.

Friends, let me tell you, this has been one of the greatest highlights of my professional career. I cannot begin to tell you how much that Facebook message meant to me.

Among the many nay-sayers, and those Chiefs' who had many more years of experience than I who told me "why are you wasting your time?" …. this message brought it all home for me. Between me and my Platoon Commander, we led this Seabee with empathy and compassion….and it paid off!! It did not come easy but in the end, we made a positive difference in this young Seabee's life and for that I will forever be grateful.

So, my friends in Corporate America, here are my thoughts, right, wrong or indifferent. When you have that one associate or team member who is always getting into some kind of trouble please remember, never give up on them and never throw in the towel.

If there is something inside of you telling you that there is more to that person than meets the eye, than take the time to counsel, coach and develop them, but never, ever give up on them. You do not know what battles or demons they are fighting. Show them empathy and compassion and give them your time, you never know the impact you may have on them. And if they choose to depart ways with your company, that is ok, you will know in your heart of hearts that you gave 120% to coach, develop and guide them. They may not openly admit it, but I guarantee you, they will appreciate your efforts and they will never forget what you did for them.

Ch.11: US Naval Academy

My Navy Seabee career is filled with many significant and defining moments for me, both personally and professionally. But there are two assignments that really gave me skills and experiences that I cherish to this day. They were both special programs assignments.

In the military there are certain assignments (tours of duty) that you must apply to and be selected for. They require special screenings and sometimes high-level clearances. Some even require oral boards where the candidate sits in front of a panel and is interviewed on their desire to get into that specific program and then drilled on their experiences and skills to ensure it is a proper fit.

The first special program assignment I was given was as the facilities operations Chief at the US Naval Academy. This served as my introduction into the profession I would pursue upon my retirement from the Navy Seabees, facilities management. I will never forget the initial conversation I had with my Detailer for this assignment, it was quite "entertaining"!

Detailing. This is a good time to talk about this process in the military. As many may know, when you serve in the military for more than one enlistment you change jobs and locations. The process of selecting your next job (tour of duty) is referred to as detailing. The detailers for the US Navy have a database that shows all available assignments (billets) for a particular rating and rank. When a Seabee of that rating and rank falls within nine months of the end of their current tour of duty they will contact the detailer to see what billets are available to them.

Now you may think that the Seabee who is up for a new tour of duty has some negotiating power in this detailing process.., *ha!*..no.., not really. It really comes down to the *needs of the Navy* and what the detailer sees as an appropriate next duty for that individual. In my case, I was eligible for shore duty.

Shore duty in the Navy refers to going to a non-deployable unit. In the Navy we have a Sea-Shore rotation to prevent (or attempt to prevent) burn out. It is not good for morale to have a Seabee do back-to-back sea tours and constantly deploy overseas. The shore duty allows the individual Seabee to "take a break" and stay in one place for a period of 2 to 3 years.

Ok, now that detailing is explained, let me go back to the conversation I had with my detailer. He told me of a couple billets he had but they did not sound interesting. I basically said, "what else you do you have?". It was at this point he said something like "well, I have this billet at the Naval Academy, but you will need to be screened for it". He went on to say he really did not know what the billet was or what I would be doing specifically. I was intrigued. Maryland sounded like a cool place to live and to be able to work at the *prestigious* US Naval Academy?... how *awesome* would that be!

The Detailer informed me that there was a point of contact that I could call to find out more about this billet. He gave me the information and I made the call. It was at this point that a Seabee Lieutenant told me that I would be overseeing the day-to-day facility operations of Bancroft Hall. He proceeded to tell me that Bancroft Hall was the largest single dormitory in the world. Well needless to say, that sealed the deal! I discussed it with Sheri and she was all for it. So I accepted orders to the United States Naval Academy and began the screening process.

Annapolis, Maryland.... wow, what a beautiful little city. If you have never been, I highly recommend! It is a sailing town, and the people are laid back and super friendly. I reported for duty and began one of the most rewarding tours of duty in my Seabee career. Bancroft Hall is *huge*, comparable to a small city in every aspect. There are medical and dental clinics, chapels, auditorium, indoor firing range, administrative offices, cobbler shop, gift store, cafes, and the list goes on and on! And as the Facility Operations Chief I interacted with every single one of those areas. It was truly a massive responsibility.

I loved the day-to-day challenges of being the Facility Operations Chief. As anyone who works in facilities management knows, no two days are ever the same! I also had a small civil servant staff that I supervised as well. These were civilians who worked for me in the facilities office. We had a gunsmith (because of the indoor firing range), a mail room lead, self-help lead, and an engraver/locksmith.

Each one of these positions were vital to the facilities support function we provided to the Midshipmen and staff. For clarification, self-help refers to the minor maintenance that Midshipmen could do on their own like changing a lightbulb or replacing a shower curtain. They could come down to our self-help office and pick up these small consumable items and do the work of replacing themselves. This allowed the facility maintenance technicians to focus on the more skilled maintenance activities required to maintain a facility of this size and magnitude like HVAC, plumbing, carpentry, etc.. All the skilled trades were represented in the maintenance organization and trust me, they were kept busy!

I have many stories and memories of my tour at the Naval Academy. My team and I supported numerous Senior Naval Officer retirements with event set up and support. Many Naval Officers who are Naval Academy graduates come back to the Naval Academy for their retirement ceremony. It was my absolute pleasure to be a part of their special day albeit "behind the scenes" and provide the proper environment for such a time-honored tradition as a US Navy retirement ceremony.

I will also say being on the Commandants staff and being a facilities manager always came with some perks. One of those being the annual Blue Angels show that would be right before graduation. We would get seats in the Commandants section, basically front and center to the air show. I cannot explain it, but we were as close to those jets flying over as we possibly could be! It made for some awesome photos and memories. My oldest son was very young at the time, but I will always remember his eyes lighting up when those jets would scream right over our heads!

Another cool opportunity that presented itself was when I was invited onto the Superintendants yacht for a cruise on the Severn river. This had more to do with the power of the Chiefs Mess then it did with my being on the Commandant staff. The Superintendants cook (a Chief) and I got to know one another through the Chiefs Initiation season. Next thing I know he is sending me an invite for a cruise on the Severn! That was a real cool experience and I was grateful for the opportunity to be on that little cruise along the river.

I also want to give a shout out to my sisters and brothers of the various Naval Academy bands. As a hobbyist drummer and music lover, I have a strong fondness to those professionals whom are blessed to make music for a living. And the professional musicians of the Naval Academy band are some of the very finest! They are all highly educated and usually have gigs with civilian bands, orchestras and symphonies. They are a very talented group of musicians and masters in their particular instrument/s of choice. If you ever visit Annapolis, Maryland during the summer, be sure to check out one of their live (and free) performances in downtown Annapolis, dockside, you will not regret it!

But among the many memories I have, perhaps the most significant is how my team and I supported the 2004 Annapolis Peace Conference. The Naval Academy was chosen as the place to host this significant event in our nation's recent history. President Bush Jr. and Secretary of State Condoleezza Rice led the conference that brought together many foreign dignitaries to discuss the way forward for the crisis in the Middle East.

You may be wondering how my facilities team and I found ourselves involved with such a significant event as this. Well, as it goes in facilities, we are the "hidden heroes". We are the ones who ensure the built environment is adequate to support such a high-profile event as the Annapolis Peace Conference. Weeks before the event I was working with the US Department of State,

Diplomatic Security Service (DSS) to iron out details of the event and identify any and all security issues. I was specifically working with a DSS Special Agent who was a former Marine Officer. I mention that he was a former Marine Officer because that comes into play with my second special programs assignment that I will speak to in the next chapter.

Nonetheless, this DSS Special Agent and I worked very closely together prior to, during and after the Annapolis Peace Conference. Because I was intimately familiar with Bancroft Hall, my facilities knowledge became crucial for him to set up his physical security team. Due to it being classified information, I cannot say too much regarding what that physical security posture looked like. However, what I will always remember is how my team and I were able to assist in providing a safe and secure environment for the conference and all attendees…that is something I will always cherish.

After the Peace Conference the DSS Special Agent wanted to hire me on the spot! I told him I was at 14 years of military service and had every intent of going to 20 years so I could obtain military retirement. He was understanding and knew he would not be able to convince me otherwise to join his team. He then said that if there was anything he could do for me, just let him know. I took advantage of his offer and asked if he had ever heard of the US Naval Support Unit, Department of State. I informed him that this was a special unit of

Navy Seabees that supported the US Department of State, Diplomatic Security Service. He let me know that he heard of them but never worked with or alongside them. We left the conversation at that.

Fast forward about six months and I received an email from the Operations Chief of the Naval Support Unit. He told me that he was contacted by a DSS Special Agent who had worked with me during the Annapolis Peace Conference. The DSS Agent told the Operations Chief that he needed to get me to the Unit. At the time I did not realize it, but this was my introduction into networking!

I will never forget the conversations the Operations Chief and I had. He was like "do you have any issues that would prevent you from obtaining a TS/SCI Clearance?" I said no. He then submitted my TS/SCI screening and after I submitted everything, I received my TS/SCI clearance. The Operations Chief called me and said that it was the fastest he had ever seen a TS/SCI clearance be granted! If memory serves me correct, my TS/SCI clearance was granted in 2 months. This is almost unheard of in the clearance world!

And so with that, we move to my second special programs assignment, The Naval Support Unit, State Department.

Ch.12: Naval Support Unit, US Department of State Diplomatic Security

I was selected for this duty in June of 2008 and reported onboard the training unit in August 2008. Training for this unit is intense and fast. First you go through anti-terrorism training and other general security awareness training. Then the technical training begins, it is approximately 2 months long. The training covers a myriad of technical security systems, both theory and application.

Upon completion of training, most Seabees are placed into the temporary duty pool out of Washington, DC. The temporary duty pool was established to provide short-term mission support globally for various Diplomatic Security Missions. This is also to keep Seabees gainfully employed until they permanently post to a US Embassy abroad for the duration of their tour of duty. If there is one thing to know about the Seabees it is you must keep them busy or they will get into shenanigans!

For Chief Petty Officers, many do not spend a lot of time in the temporary duty pool as they normally get posted soon thereafter graduating technical training or better yet, they know prior to graduating from technical school their assignment abroad.

My posting assignment is a story in itself, and once again, Sheri played a big part in it!

The Assistant Officer-in-Charge of Naval Support Unit State Department was a Master Chief. Prior to my transfer to technical training when the family and I were still stationed at the Naval Academy in Annapolis, Maryland, the Master Chief asked me to come to the Naval Support Unit headquarters to discuss my posting assignment. I told Sheri about the future meeting and she immediately said she wanted to be there. This caught me off guard and I was adamant that this was a military meeting and she could not be present. Well, in true Sheri form, she was persistent and insisted she go with me…, I reluctantly obliged.

The day had arrived. Sheri and I headed from Arnold, Maryland to Rosslyn, Virginia to meet with the Master Chief. We arrived early in the morning and shared some coffee. The Master Chief then proceeded to tell us that he had two options for our posting: Bangkok, Thailand or

Frankfurt, Germany.

Well, I do not think I need to tell you which one Sheri and I were most excited about. Master Chief discussed the two locations, explaining a bit about the cultures and the countries. Then he said something that Sheri immediately latched onto. He said that the Chief Petty Officer-in-Charge at Frankfurt, Germany had an additional duty and one that was not to be taken lightly. He stated that Frankfurt, Germany was where the annual Seabee Ball for the Naval Support Unit State Department was held. He proceeded to state the importance of being able to fundraise and host the annual Seabee Ball. He needed to ensure that whichever Chief he posted there, that Chief could carry out the additional responsibilities of organizing, fundraising, and being the Master-of-Ceremonies for the Seabee Ball.

Sheri immediately put on her charm and assured Master Chief that I could handle this without fail. Well, he must have been impressed because he instantly made the decision to post us to Frankfurt right there on the spot! I did not say two words this entire time yet the Master Chief decided we would be posted to Frankfurt.., all thanks to Sheri and her charm! What an absolutely crazy day that was. And rest assured, Sheri has never let it rest. Perhaps one of the best assignments in State Department, Frankfurt, Germany.., and Sheri was the one who got us there, no doubt about it!

Engineering Services Center (ESC) Frankfurt. This US Consulate is the largest in State Department and the ESC covers the largest geographical region for the Diplomatic Security Service. The Engineering Services Center supports seventy-two Embassies and Consulates across the EURASIAN region and at anytime, any of these facilities could call us for technical security systems field support. Our travel requirement was about 85%. It was crazy how much we traveled in a given year to support the Diplomatic Mission. And when we were not traveling, my office of Seabees and our spouses were planning and executing fundraising activities to support the annual Seabee Ball.

Sheri and I had huge ambitions on the Seabee Ball for each year we were there. We were adamant to make them memorable for the Diplomats and the Seabees. But to do this, we had to fundraise a substantial amount of money. On average, it would cost us $15,000 for a Seabee Ball. Honestly, we knew we could have done it much cheaper if we chose venues with much less "prestige", but that was not our style.

The first Seabee Ball we hosted together was at a Castle, the Ronneburg Castle to be exact. Wow, what an experience! We had planned it to be a medieval dinner and entertainment experience mixed with the formal Seabee Military traditions. I will never forget when Sheri and I arrived a few hours before the event. Being the

Master-of-Ceremonies, I always made it a point to get to the venue hours before the start of the Ball to check-in and ensure everything was setup as planned. While Sheri and I were looking to ensure nameplates were set out on the head table, the Seabee Ball sign was in place, and all the other Seabee Ball decorations were in order, Sheri noticed there was no silverware at the place settings. She turned to me and asked "where is the silverware"?

We immediately went to the staff and asked why there was no silverware. They explained that this was to be a medieval dinner and back in those times everyone ate with their hands! Well, although this sounded cool as hell, we had to remember that the military guests were going to be in full dress uniforms and the spouses would be in ball gowns and tuxedos. We politely informed the staff that we would need proper silverware for this event and thankfully they understood.

The night went without fail and so many awesome memories were made. But that was just the first Seabee Ball we hosted!

The next year and final Seabee Ball that Sheri and I would host, we really wanted to kick it up a few notches. I asked one of the civilians we worked with who had been living in Germany for a number of years for any recommendations. He told me that we should do the Seabee Ball in a Palace, or in German, a Schloss. Schloss Philippsruhe was the venue he recommended.

I went home that evening and talked it over with Sheri. We looked up the Schloss on line and immediately knew that we had to have the Seabee Ball at this beautiful venue. We started making plans and contacted the Schloss over the next few days to start planning the event.

This Seabee Ball would be a little different than the previous one regarding my professional development. This year we were going to host the US Consul General of Frankfurt, Germany. The Naval Support Unit Officer-in-Charge contacted me and stated they wanted to have an executive luncheon with the Consul General prior to the Seabee Ball. It was on me to plan and lead an executive luncheon with the Consul General and some Navy VIP's. Needless to say, these were uncharted waters for me.

Planning an event like this took some research. I had to review protocols and etiquette to ensure all were followed diligently. There are specific protocols when it comes to civilians, foreign service officers, and military officers when they are all together that I needed to learn. Being that I was not a military Officer, this was all new to me. In the military we have a duty for Officers, they are called Protocol Officers. I never really knew what that meant or what they did but this executive luncheon gave me a little taste of it!

All in all, the luncheon went great and there was a lot of great conversation and knowledge sharing. We all learned something from one another during that lunch, it was an experience I will not soon forget.

The Seabee Ball itself was in my honest opinion, the best one yet! I do not know if it was because Sheri and I knew this was the last one we would be leading or what, but the atmosphere was off the charts. We had a great number of Seabees and their spouses come in for the Ball, much more than the previous year. One of the Seabee's volunteered to DJ the entire night as well and he did an excellent job! As for Sheri, she was in her element. She wore a beautiful purple ball gown and had a tiara that she wore the entire night. She was definitely the Queen Bee this night!

Beside the fundraising and hosting of the annual Seabee Ball, my Seabees and I supported a ton of Diplomatic Missions throughout EURASIA. I will never forget one mission we had. We were tasked to perform some classified construction for a senior dignitary. Since this was a classified area, we had no details on who worked in this area because we did not have a need to know. However, on the first day of construction we were directed to leave about mid-day for about one and a half hours. The person giving us this direction stated that once a week a call had to be made to the President of the United States (POTUS) and we would have to leave and come back later.

How crazy is that?! We were not informed of this until the project started. Luckily, it did not negatively impact our construction schedule and in true Seabee fashion, we still completed the project ahead of schedule. But seriously, you cannot make this kind of stuff up. We had to leave the job site so a call could be made to POTUS.., cool but crazy.

There is another story that I am reminded of during my tour in Germany with the Department of State. This one was another one of those stories where I found myself in a challenging leadership position.

My team and I were tasked with decommissioning a SCIF (Sensitive Compartmented Information Facility). Well, as the demolition began my First Class Petty Officer on the job noticed that the floor tiles were sized at 6 inches by 6 inches and that raised a red flag with him. He had a concern that this size floor tile was an indicator that it was ACM..Asbestos Containing Material. He immediately made the decision to stop work and subsequently informed me of his concern.

As the Chief Petty Officer in Charge, I was the senior leader and had to take his concern seriously. I immediately called back to my boss and informed him of our findings. Well, this news was not taken positively and he was not convinced that our assumptions were substantiated. He insisted that we continue with the demolition phase in order to stay on schedule for the project. I pushed back and asked if we could get the tiles tested. From what I was seeing, no one had ever had this type of issue before so no one really knew where to go or who to contact for addressing the issue. I do not put any blame on my boss, no one ever encountered a situation like this and we were all just trying to decide how best to move forward.

After a lot of back and forth on the phone, and finding out who needed to be informed, we got the approval to test the tiles for ACM. A few days later the testing was completed and sure enough it was positive for asbestos. We mutually decided that we would leave the floor tiles in place and not disturb them as we took down the rest of the SCIF.

This is just another one of those stories of leadership and doing the right thing in the face of adversity. I will not get into details but I will say that I faced some pretty serious resistance when I mentioned the concern of ACM. I had some people thinking I was making a mountain of a molehill and that it was not that big of a deal. But I knew in my heart of hearts that we needed to at least take the precautionary measures to ensure the safety of the decommissioning crew. Looking back, I am glad that I stopped work as it prevented unwanted exposure to asbestos. And at the end of the day, it was proven that the tiles were ACM as my First Class Petty Officer alluded to.

As a leader and irregardless of opposition, you must remain steadfast to your beliefs and you must take your team seriously when they bring forth concerns. The "easy" thing for me to have done in this situation would have been to say something like "suck it up Seabee, just get the job done". But I knew in my heart of hearts that my Seabee brought something up that needed addressed and not swept under the rug and that is exactly what I did.

***

It was nearing the time to call my detailer for my next duty assignment. I figured I would be going back to a deployable unit, more than likely, back to a Naval Mobile Construction Battalion aka "the green machine". However, the Assistant Officer-in-Charge of the Naval Support Unit contacted me and asked if I was interested in being the Naval Support Unit Operations Chief. This position is based out of Washington, DC and is high profile. I conferred with Sheri and we decided what the heck, let's go back to the East Coast so we could live in Annapolis again. Needless to say, we really love the Annapolis, Maryland area.

So, around July of 2011 we transferred from Frankfurt, Germany to Washington, DC where I took over Naval Support Unit Global Operations. This role was very unique to NSU State Department. I had a lot of authority, more so than a typical Chief Petty Officer. I also gained a lot of exposure to the broader Diplomatic Security Organization and other Branches of the Federal Government.

There were a ton of Diplomatic Security missions we supported globally. Unfortunately, most of it cannot be spoke about because it is all classified. However, one significant team I oversaw was a high-profile special team of Seabee Security Technical Specialists who deployed to high threat areas on a 6-month rotation. This special team of Seabees performed unique technical security system installs and maintenance for a specific application. These Seabees were hand-selected and were truly the cream of the crop of the Unit. There were many situations where they had to use their "Can Do" ingenuity to solve complex technical security system issues in the field.

I cannot state enough how important this field support team was to the Diplomatic Security Service mission in high-risk areas of the world. The team had their challenges but they performed their duties flawlessly and through their efforts directly supported the safety and security of high profile Diplomats overseas.

As the Naval Support Unit Operations Chief, I was involved with all matters of the Unit. I also had the Regional Chief Petty Officers-in-Charge (CPOIC) reporting into me. These Regional CPOIC's were located globally in each operating region of the US Department of State so one of the biggest challenges was communication. When you manage and lead teams across time zones (and across the globe), it is always a challenge to find a time where everyone can meet. We would have monthly meetings to discuss regional issues and overall morale of the Seabees and how they were adjusting to living and working within the Foreign Service.

I cannot stress enough the challenges of this Unit

for the Seabees assigned. We are taken away from a known environment (Seabees) and put into this new and different world of Foreign Service. Many Seabees communicate directly with Senior Foreign Service Officers and sometimes with members of the Senior Executive Service (SES). These customers can be demanding and they all want something, be it more cameras, better technical security systems, etc.. Our Seabees have to navigate those conversations with tact and Diplomacy (pun intended). It is definitely a different mindset and one has to adjust their communication style to better acclimate to their environment.

This was actually one of the topics I would discuss during the onboarding process of new Seabees to the Unit. I knew that these Seabees were smart and had the hard, technical skills to do the job. But, what they needed to understand were the soft skills that were needed to professionally communicate to the customers, who were mainly Foreign Service Officers. This is actually no different then anyone wanting to pursue a career in facilities management to be honest. In facilities management, we get the same type of thing, everyone wants something from us but we may not always have the money or the solution. We have to learn to navigate those conversations with tact and (yep, you guessed it)... Diplomacy.

Another cool aspect of the role I had in Washington, DC was leading the recruiting efforts for the Unit.

Each training class we had a goal of so many Seabees (students) that would need to be in the class. We were held to making that goal by State Department because it was their instructors who taught the classes. State Department always wanted to ensure the class sizes were max'd out. It was my responsibility to ensure we met the class quotas without fail.

We had our usual Seabee bases that we would travel to on a routine basis to give the Naval Support Unit presentation and scout for candidates. But, I also knew that there was an untapped pool of Seabees stationed at other military installations across the United States. I performed some market research and identified a few other military installations that I would travel to and give our presentation. By widening the market we were recruiting from, we were able to increase the candidate pool significantly. This helped us to achieve and exceed class quotas consistently.

Running global operations is not easy and it is very demanding and stressful. I always had my phone on me, 24/7, and it never failed that I would receive phone calls from around the world day in and day out. Sheri was very understanding and as always, she supported me and understood what we did to support the US Department of State Diplomatic Security mission.

Friends I cannot overstate it enough, if you have a spouse, you need to ensure that as a couple, you support one another. This is not a one-sided relationship, it takes sacrifice and understanding on both sides to make marriage and life work. And if either of you happen to work in a high operational tempo, high stress occupation, the support of your spouse is absolutely crucial to your well-being.

I enjoyed this special program tour of duty, it was an awesome feeling knowing what my teams and I did to support and service Diplomats around the world! But, it was also going to be my last tour of duty in the military.., I decided to retire from the Navy Seabees in 2013.

It was "just time"...

Ch.13: Transition To Civilian World

While one is serving their Country in the military, they always wonder and ask, "how will I know when it is time to hang up our Nations Cloth for the last time?". And the many people whom I asked this question of during my own military career always gave me this same answer.., "you will just know". It never really sank in and I never fully understood what they meant by that answer, but nonetheless, I would heed their advice.

Fast forward to the year 2012 and that is exactly how it played out for me. As I spoke about in the previous chapter, family and I were stationed in Washington, DC on a special programs assignment with the US Department of State, Diplomatic Security. I was the Operations Chief for our 90-person unit where I led global field operations in support of Diplomatic Security Missions abroad. This special program assignment was one of the most rewarding of my military career. Being able to support Diplomacy around the world was and always will be one of the greatest blessings I had in my career. However, it was also high operational tempo and extremely stressful. As is typical of any Operations Lead role, I was on call 24/7/365 and always had my work phone attached to the hip.

This environment started to take its toll on my mind and on the family. Maybe looking back in hindsight it was a little emotional but, I literally woke up on a Monday and during the train ride into the office I decided right then and there that I was going to submit my retirement papers. I went into the office and immediately submitted my Transfer to the Fleet Reserve paperwork aka retirement papers. I informed my Senior Chief and of course he supported my decision.

Then came the dreadful phone call to Sheri. I called her up and said, "I am retiring". She instantly replied with "yes I know, in a couple of years". You see, we had every intention of going to 25 years of service and that was the plan as Sheri knew it. But me, in my sometimes reactive and instantaneous decisiveness made the immediate decision at 23 years to hang up the uniform. Needless to say, I received an earful on the phone call that lasted about 15 minutes (but it seemed like an hour)!

There are some things I have done in my career that I wish I would have done better, this was one of them. Conferring with Sheri on such a big decision as retiring from the military was something I should have done. Instead, I dropped my papers and informed her after the fact. This was not a very strategic nor smart move on my part and in hindsight, I showed great disrespect to Sheri by not having her be a part of such a significant life decision that would not only impact me, but our entire family. However, as Sheri always does (and after she gave me an earful) she simply said "well, I guess we are retiring".

If there is one theme in my life it is God seemingly always puts a ton of things on my plate, many times all at once. My choosing to retire from the military was no different. At this time in my life, I was attending the University of Maryland Global Campus (previously known as the University of Maryland University College) and was two classes away from graduating with my Bachelor of Science, Environmental Management degree. I knew that we had to start planning our move from Washington, DC to Chicago, Illinois. I also had to start figuring out my post-military career and how to obtain that employment immediately upon my retirement from the Seabees because quite honestly, the bills would not stop coming in.

With those things hanging over my head, there was yet another "surprise" awaiting me that I did not see coming. I will never forget about 1-2 weeks after I told Sheri about my retiring what happened next. It was a Sunday morning and Sheri and I were having our usual morning chat. Then out of the blue she said "Randy, I have that feeling I had with Nathen, I need to take a test".

"The test" for those who are not familiar is the pregnancy test...one line negative, two lines positive. And sure enough, two lines showed on the stick and we found out Sheri was pregnant with our third child. As if I did not have enough to worry about, now we had a baby on the way!

To put this all into perspective..., I had two classes to complete for my degree, we had to start planning our move back to Illinois, I had to obtain employment in Illinois (where I had no professional network established), and now we had a third baby on the way.... wow, that was a lot. I felt overwhelmed and told Sheri I was not going back to college until after we moved, I had a job, and we were settled in. Sheri immediately said "there is no way I am going to let you stop now. If you stop now, you may never get the opportunity again and I will not let you live your life saying, 'I was two classes away from obtaining my degree'". So, I did not drop out and instead completed those last two classes. It was not easy, and I lived on caffeine and little sleep for a few months, but I got it done.

With all those things on my shoulders, Sheri kept encouraging me saying that God never gives us more then we can handle. And that proved once again to be true because we did get through it all, relatively unscathed.

It was definitely a trying and stressful time, especially when I was not getting called for job interviews. If there is one thing I believe many veterans struggle with it is not getting those calls for interviews. We have a strong pride in ourselves and when we apply to jobs that we believe are the perfect fit for us and do not get the subsequent call for interview, we get discouraged.

But, before I continue with my transition story, I would be remiss if I did not speak to my military retirement ceremony itself because it was pretty cool. One thing about the Navy Seabees is we always take care of each other. This proved to be the case when I reached out to a fellow Seabee Chief who was stationed at Great Lakes, Illinois. I had this awesome idea that I would end my career where it all began, at Great Lakes Naval Base. To go back to the place that I became a sailor way back in 1990 to retire, how cool would that be! Well in true Seabee Can Do spirit, this awesome friend and fellow Utilitiesman Chief came through for Sheri and I and reserved one of the ceremonial halls at Great Lakes for my retirement ceremony.

And what a ceremony it was! It was not huge, but we had just enough family and friends attend to make it a retirement I will never forget. I had another idea as well. I figured since Sheri and I were turning over a new leaf so to speak by leaving the military and going forward with our next chapter, why not renew our wedding vows? I reached out to Father Kevin who was our priest for our wedding and he happily obliged to perform our renewal.

So after the military retirement ceremony, Sheri and I renewed our vows in front of friends, family, shipmates and Seabees. What an awesome memory!

I also remember another interesting event that happened and it was completely unexpected. I believe I was in the middle of my retirement speech when I heard some commotion toward the back of the room. I had no idea what was happening but I started seeing this surge of excitement come over one of the Seabees who was in attendance.

Well, as it were, right then and there as I was giving my retirement speech the results for those selected to Chief Petty Officer were announced. And low and behold, one of the Seabees in attendance was selected for Chief! What was even more ironic is that the picture on the front cover of this book was taken at my retirement ceremony. Although you cannot see him in the picture, the First Class Petty Officer (UT1) to whom I am rendering a salute was the one selected to Chief! How cool is that?

I want to say that the US Navy is the only branch of service that has a time-honored tradition of holding retirement ceremonies. We go above and beyond to send our Sailors and Seabees ashore for the last time with this time honored ceremony. It is strictly voluntary to the servicemember if they want to have a retirement ceremony or not, but most choose to have it. I am so glad that I chose to have a retirement ceremony, and again, to be able to do it at the place where it all began 23 years earlier was just icing on the cake!

I want to speak more about the transition and my personal experience as I had many lessons learned over my first 3 years post-military. The first lesson I had to learn was keeping my ego in check! I cannot tell you how many conversations Sheri had with me telling me that my ego needed to be knocked off my shoulder. At the time, I did not understand what she was telling me.

This is how I saw myself:

- I was a Chief Petty Officer in the Navy Seabees.

- I was a facility operations manager for the world's largest single dormitory in the world at the US Naval Academy which was considered a special program / tour of duty.

- I served 5 years on another special program supporting the US Department of State, Diplomatic Security.

I truly felt my crap did not stink and that employers would be knocking down doors to hire me...

I was wrong, dead wrong.

I had so much to learn about what one has to do to become a professional in the corporate world of work. I did attend TAP (Transition Assistance Program) in Washington, DC and that was a great informational course. I know many of my sisters and brothers had a bad experience with their TAP class, but mine was really done well. Perhaps it was because it was in Washington, DC and most of the attendees were senior military Officers. The course was geared toward preparing the students for executive / senior management roles. I am grateful for that TAP class as it taught me a lot regarding gaining a management position in Corporate.

My first job interview experience was crazy. I was making connections and building my network on LinkedIn. As things started to gain momentum and I learned how to really use LinkedIn, I started making connections with other Seabees in the Chicago area. One connection I made was with a retired Civil Engineer Corps Officer (Seabee) who was the Vice President of Facilities and Administration at the Illinois Institute of Technology. One trend that is prevalent among US Navy Seabee Officers is many of them obtain high ranking positions in the facilities department of higher education institutions upon their retirement from the Navy Seabees.

This connection proved to be invaluable because it led to my first job interview post-Seabees. He reached out to me about a role on his team that he knew with my Seabee experience and being a retired Chief, I would be a perfect fit. Family and I were still living in Maryland at this time, so he had planned to fly me to the Illinois Institute of Technology Campus in Chicago for the job interview. Let me tell you, this was one crazy and very long day!

His Office Administrator booked me a red eye flight so that I would arrive in Chicago by 6AM. I believe I woke up to get to airport around 3AM and then slept on the short plane ride to Chicago. When I arrived in Chicago, I went to my inlaws who live near the airport. We agreed beforehand that I could borrow one of their cars for the interview. I freshened up a bit at my inlaws home and then jumped in the car and drove to the IIT campus. My interview start time was 8:30AM.

I arrived at the interview location, checked in and was immediately brought into a room to begin the interview. This interview process lasted the better part of a day. I think I was interviewing for about 7 hours total!! We started at 8:30AM and ended around 3:00PM. The Retired Seabee Officer was the last one I interviewed with. He wanted to keep going with the interview but knew I had a flight to catch. If I did not have that flight to catch, I have no idea how much longer past 3:00PM that interview would have gone with him.

For my first post-Seabee job interview, I was overwhelmed to say the least. No one ever spoke about interviews lasting 7 hours long! Part of the interview process was speaking with the Human Resources representative. He spoke to me about benefits and other compensation related items. I thought this was a bit odd that he would be sharing HR information before I was extended a job offer. But then again, I was also excited because I had assumed I was going to get said offer.

Well, unfortunately that is not what had happened. After about a week had passed, I received the dreaded rejection email. You know the one... it usually starts off with "we regret to inform you..." as soon as you read that you know you did not get the job. So, I interviewed with numerous personnel at IIT for a period of 7 hours. I also went to lunch with some of the folks I would be working with in that role. The lunch seemed to go really well also. But, after all that time and effort for all involved, I did not get the job. I was frustrated and aggravated.

I believe many veterans can relate to this. We are so used to being successful in every mission we undertake that when we are rejected for a job, it hits, and it hits hard. I kept reliving the interview in my head trying to figure out what mistakes I had made. What did I not say that I could have that may have made for a better outcome? I was beating myself up for weeks afterward, it was not a good time for me. At the time I just did not understand that everything in our lives is led by God. God had closed this door for a reason, I just could not understand what that reason was.

But it worked out because after a few weeks of sulking I received a call from a recruiter for a job at another company. I distinctly remember this day. Family and I were at Culver's getting ready to sit down for lunch when I received a phone call from an unknown number. I usually ignore unknown numbers for fear of spam but when you are applying for jobs, it behoove you to answer all calls (you never know if it is spam or a recruiter). This call was indeed a recruiter. He told me of a position he had for a service manager. We made some small talk and after hearing a little more about the role I told him I was interested. We scheduled a follow-up call at a more convenient time and date.

We had a proper phone screening a few days later. I was then asked to provide a couple professional references in which I did, promptly. The one reference was a Security Engineering Officer (SEO) I had worked with in Frankfurt, Germany during my tour with the US Department of State. I do not know what he said or how he said it, but he literally sealed the deal to move forward in the interview process!

The recruiter set up a face-to-face interview at the company headquarters. I remember this interview a little vaguely. I know it lasted about an hour...much shorter than my previous experience at Illinois Institute of Technology that is for sure! The very next day I was made an offer. I did not know it at the time but to have this quick of a turnaround on a job offer is a bit rare in corporate America. I accepted the offer and bada bing, bada boom, I had my first job post-Seabees...I was elated!!

This first job post-Seabees was one hell of a wakeup call for me and quite the learning curve. You have to remember that I was coming off a special programs tour with the US Department of State, so my mindset was still very much high operational tempo. I was still acting as "The Chief". I expected things to happen in short order and I expected my team to execute their work without question. Well, you can only imagine how that went!

***

Allow me to talk a little about leadership out here in Corporate America. One thing I hear and see a lot on social media is the messaging of "hire a veteran, they are leaders"! I am not saying veterans are not leaders, however, the leadership style and how it is used in the military is different than in the civilian world. Although many do not use their rank to get their troops to execute work i.e., "I am the Chief and I said to do it so do it", we must keep in mind that there is still the underlying notion that military members execute work from their superiors without question. This is military discipline 101. So even though we do not outright say it or apply it, the troops will do what we ask of them just because of the rank we wear on our collar irregardless of them having respect for us as an individual.

Out here in corporate things do not work this way. You cannot come into an organization and say something like "just do it because I am your boss"! That is a sure-fire way to lose your team to another company or department. You will instantly demotivate them and they will not lift a finger for you for anything. And quite honestly, one of my civilian bosses that I had did this to me almost verbatim. Needless to say I ended up leaving the firm not long thereafter.

So, without the rank, it takes a different course of action to motivate your team and allow them to execute the taskings at hand. It takes a different approach to leadership, and it is one that can only really be learned through trial and error.

This is why I say that having military leadership is an asset but do not think your military style of leadership will help you to be successful in corporate. You must adjust fire on your leadership style and adjust to your new environment. It is not easy to explain, you just have to live through it and like I said earlier, have some trial and error before you get it "right".

Enough on that topic, let's return to that first job I had post-Seabees. What a bad ass job it was! In a nutshell, my team and I worked around trains and trucks, how cool is that? We supported the intermodal industry and 4 of the 5 Class I Railroads nationwide and including Canada. The systems we maintained were really cool. They were remote inspection systems and automated gate controllers. In a nutshell, the systems took camera photos of the container trucks that came onto an intermodal yard. This was to inspect for and electronically document damages, proper placement of hazardous materials markings, etc...

The next part of our system was the automated gate control system. This is essentially similar to the old tollway systems that had gate arms that would open and close to allow vehicles to pass after toll payment was made. But our system was to monitor and control access into the intermodal yard. It used biometrics to "read-in" a driver. It would then tell the driver where to drop off or pick up their container in the yard.

If you have never been to an intermodal yard, all I can say is they are massive! And there are containers stacked three high everywhere so as you drive on these intermodal yards it is easy to lose your bearings on where you are going. Then there are hostler drivers moving containers all over the yard. They drive relentlessly to get these containers to their locations. Needless to say, you have to have your eyes focused everywhere because of all the activity happening on the yard. It is kind of controlled chaos honestly.

I cannot speak in detail about the systems my team and I maintained because they are proprietary. But I will say, they were all computer-controlled so the company I worked for was a technology company. Yes, that is right, this old crusty Navy Seabee worked with a bunch of IT Professionals! It was definitely a bit of a different environment for me that is for sure.

One thing I learned fast, cursing was not necessarily embraced at this company. And quite frankly, now that I have held quite a few jobs at different companies, I can honestly say this is across all industries. Again, as a veteran, I have had to make these "little" adjustments. Still to this day I find myself cursing, it is something with which I will always struggle. But I try each day to do better, that is all you can really do...*strive to do better.*

That first job post service was a blessing. I was one of the first veterans hired to the company and my boss never worked with a veteran before. He did not have any military in his family either, so it was a learning experience for both of us. He was patient with me and gave me sound advice at times when I would lose my composure or do and/or say something stupid. Although, at the time, I sometimes resisted his advice. I still had a bit of an ego…. I was a Navy Chief, remember?! Ugh, if I could only go back in time and knock that ego off my shoulders.

I was also unfairly judgmental during my first job post-Seabees and I am ashamed to admit that. My boss was a Director and I had this preconceived notion of what a Director should know. I would get frustrated when he would ask me questions that I "thought" a Director should already know. Looking back, I was a bit of a jerk to him at times and it was totally uncalled for. Again, it came back to my own ego and being a bit arrogant. We live and we learn.

***

Let me tell you about one story that was a huge lost opportunity for me. The company I worked for was small, we had about two hundred employees at the time I worked there. The President would always be walking the offices and talking with everyone, he was very personable.

It was around noon. I went to the lunchroom to grab a bite to eat. The President came out of nowhere and started talking with me. Eventually the conversation turned to "hey you want to go play a round of golf with me?" I told him that I couldn't because I was the service manager and it was my job to ensure that the systems stayed up and running. It was my belief that I had *no time* to play golf, I had to *be there* for my team and customers. I *refused* to play golf with the President of the company, wow..., looking back, I was so naïve!!!

Needless to say, when I arrived home and told Sheri what had happened, well, let's just say she gave me an earful. She was like how the heck could you pass up one-on-one time with the President of the company? He did not want to just play golf, he wanted to hear from you! You could have established a solid relationship with him and who knows what that could have resulted in. You just passed up a huge opportunity that you will never get again.

I think you get the picture, she read me the riot act!

But this was my thinking at the time. I had *no time* for small talk around a coffee pot, I had *no time* to play golf, I was there *to do a job* and do it well. I was the field services manager, I worked in operations…. *"ops never stops"* was my motto. I just could not peel myself away, my job was *too "vital" to the mission* to do that. I think many veterans struggle with this when they first leave the service and work in Corporate. We are always about getting the job done and not BS'ing with our peers, there just *is not any time* for that in our minds.

Well, to my fellow veterans, there is *always* time for that! Please do not make those same mistakes I have made; it will only hinder you and your career growth post-service. Who knows how my career trajectory may have gone had I went golfing that day; I will never know.

After a year had passed it was time for my annual performance review. I remember getting all my facts and notes together in typical military fashion to demonstrate all I had done over the course of the year. I received a solid review and was happy with it. But there was something else that came about during that review that I was not too happy about. I will not divulge the details because this company treated me well and I have no ill-will toward them. However, I left my review in an emotional state.

I was aggravated and upset. I kept thinking of all I had done over the course of the year and could not understand what had happened. It was during this emotional state that I would make a misstep in my career and learned an important lesson about making emotional rather than strategic decisions.

***

I was cold called by a military recruiter about 48 hours after my annual performance review. Military recruiters are recruiters who specifically target military veterans. They themselves are usually veterans so they get these kind of recruiting jobs to continue their service. It is commendable but some do not always have the candidate's best interests front and center.

This recruiter called me about an Area Operations Manager role for a well-known facilities services company. I was interested because up to this point, I had not had the opportunity to get into facilities management. Ever since my facilities operations role at the Naval Academy, it was my goal to be a facilities manager post-Seabees. So, when I was contacted about this role, I figured it would be my shoe-in for facilities management. I expressed my interest and the recruiter lined up the interview.

Up to this point things were going good in the process. However, on the day of my interview things took a turn for the worse. I remember arriving to the interview location around 9:00AM. There was no reception desk, so I looked around for someone to speak to. Finally, someone came out and asked who I was and what I was there for. I politely explained I was there for an interview. This person looked a bit startled and said they would be right back. They then disappeared for about 15 minutes. *Red flag #1.*

Finally, for what seemed like an eternity to me, a group of three people came out and greeted me. I could tell they were unsure of what position I was there to interview for. *Red flag #2.*

The interview itself was rocky and uncomfortable. They asked some general questions regarding my background and experience. They then asked if I had questions. I proceeded to ask them some questions, but many they did not have answers to. *Red flag #3.*

The interview concluded in what I remember to be about 30 to 45 minutes. I left a bit dumbfounded. I immediately called the recruiter and told him about the interview. He re-assured me and said he would get back to me with any next steps. In about 3 days, I received a verbal offer and accepted.

You may be wondering why I accepted after the three red flags. You may be thinking "are you crazy Randy?" Well, as I had stated earlier, I was in an emotional state. I was not thinking clearly. What makes this situation even worse is when I told Sheri what had happened during the interview, she said that she did not have a good feeling about the job and I should not take it. But me being the stubborn one, I did not listen to Sheri and convinced myself that this was the job for me!

Two weeks into the job I was already editing my resume and putting myself back out on the market. Yes, it did not take long for me to realize this was a bad career move. Fortunately, after 6 months working an astronomical number of hours per week, I was offered a facilities manager job with another company and I submitted my resignation. The resignation was not well-received by my boss. He tried many tactics to try and get me to stay but I knew that it just would not work out and explained that to him. He was disheartened but ultimately understood my decision.

This was a hard lesson for me, but it shouldn't have been. As we say in the military, my spidey-senses were in overdrive during the recruiting and interview process. Looking back there were so many warning signs that I just flat out ignored.

The recruiter was moving fast and was not clear on the job from the outset.

The recruiter could not give me good information on the company.

There were all the red flags during the face-to-face

interview.

Most importantly, there was Sheri, telling me that she did not feel good about the job. If there is one thing I should have known by now it is..., *always listen to your spouse!* I did not listen to Sheri and it bit me in the backside, big time!

However, there is always a positive side to anything in life and there were some positives with this job. I met some amazing Union Custodians that worked tirelessly at the schools. It is definitely a thankless job and I have always had great respect for those who choose this profession, especially in the K-12 environment. I also learned a lot about advances in cleaning methods and technology, floor care and maintenance (especially specialized floor care like concrete and terrazzo), and H2O cleaning solutions. That last one is really cool. H2O cleaning solutions is a system that converts water into cleaning solutions that can be used for general cleaning and disinfecting. It is environmentally friendly and sustainable. I learned many skills around environmental services (janitorial) that I still apply to this day, and for that, I am grateful.

***

After that job and as I had stated earlier, I took my first job as a facilities manager in corporate world. I really enjoyed this position and the people I served and worked with on a day-to-day basis. I was the first onsite facility manager for this location so there were some apprehensions on the part of the client at first. As it goes in outsourced professional services, one must establish themselves and earn the trust and confidence of the client. *This does not always come easy!*

But in true *Can Do* fashion, I established myself and I did earn that trust and confidence. So much so that I truly became a part of the team in those offices I worked in and supported. I have so many great memories of all those I supported during this facility manager role. The company/client I supported had a fantastic culture. Everyone was like a family and once I earned their trust, I was just as much a part of their family as anyone. I never felt like a contractor or a service provider, I always felt and was treated as part of their team. For that I am forever grateful.

But as it goes in outsourced services, we were coming to the final year of the contract and we were not sure if it would be renewed. I was really stressed out. I had worked in this role for just over two years and the work environment was second to none and I did not want to leave!

I remember many nights praying and talking to Sheri about what was happening. And the friends I had made with many of my co-workers were also concerned. None of them wanted to see me go. But sometimes this is what happens when you work in the outsourcing profession.

My intuition came to fruition and we were told our contract was not going to be renewed. This news hit like a ton of bricks. My co-workers (now friends) were upset. They were all praying for me and helping me with finding a new job. Again, this team I worked with and supported were just awesome. They even took me out for lunch on my last day, it was so special!

If any of you from this awesome team are reading this book (you know who you are)…, I want you to know that I will always be grateful for your friendship and support, you all are the best!

For those reading this book who work in outsourced services, you know how rare it is when the client you support truly takes you in and makes you a part of their team. The environment I worked in was truly *one of a kind.* I learned so much supporting this particular client (a technology company), with many in the offices I supported working in high value technology sales. As the saying goes, if you want to succeed, surround yourself with successful people. Everyone I supported as their facility manager I respected and valued. And once I opened up and started having conversations with many of them, the more I realized something about civilians and veterans. *They (civilians) are just as interested in what we (veterans) did as we are interested in what they do.*

So with that I want to leave a message to any veteran

reading this book. Have those conversations, share your stories, and *be curious* about your co-workers. Ask them about their careers, ask them what they did to get to where they are, and always have an open mind.

One thing I despise is the *"us against them"* mentality that is still prevalent in corporate America with "us" being "the veteran" and "them" being "the civilian". We have had different life experiences, there is no denying, but neither is better than the other. We can always learn from one another if we just keep an open mind and are open to conversation.

***

I hold no doubt in my mind that God had His hands in my future when I received the message that we lost that contract. It was not easy and I was stressed, but I always had faith that God would put me where I needed to be. How did He do it? Well, when I found out we had lost that contract, I also discovered that my current firm was the company who won the business! This was all in God's plan, there is no doubt about it.

A little backstory on the firm I currently work for at the time of this writing:

I started researching Corporate Real Estate Services companies and Facilities Services companies when I was still serving in the Navy Seabees in 2012. I was always attracted to this particular firm because of their strong brand and their culture. A few months prior to my retirement from the Navy Seabees, I applied to dozens of roles with the firm but never received or went any further than the initial phone screen. It was frustrating. With my facilities management experience from the US Naval Academy, I could not understand why I never made it far into the interview process.

It was not until years later (2017 to be exact) that things finally fell into place. I was contacted by a recruiter with this firm and we had a pleasant conversation. This was unlike all previous conversations I had with recruiters. This recruiter and I literally had a "get to know each other" call, that was it. They did not have a current role in mind at the time, they just wanted to get to know me and learn about where I wanted to go with my career. This was such a relaxing and genuine conversation, I truly appreciated this approach. They told me they would send out my resume to the entire recruiting team at the firm and see where things may land.

It was just a month or two later that I received a cold call from a hiring manager who wanted to interview me for an open role on their team with this firm. I was elated and relieved! This was finally my opportunity to obtain employment with this well-known firm. All went well and I was hired in November 2017, just a few days before my birthday…, the perfect birthday present!

As I had mentioned earlier, I had been applying to this specific firm since 2012 but never received so much as a phone screen. But I never gave up! So the lesson here for all of you reading is, be persistent. If you are strongly attracted to a specific company and have a strong desire to work for said company, keep applying. Do not lose faith, do not give up. If it is meant to be, it will be..., God-willing!

I have had a rollercoaster ride post-Seabees as I navigated my corporate career. But looking back, I know God put me in all these different roles for all the right reasons. I needed time to rediscover who I am and not define myself by what I did. I also needed time to decompress.

Coming off duty with the Department of State, I was at a high operational tempo mindset. I needed time to slow down, relax, and learn the ropes. This did not come easy for me but after quite a few years I have finally slowed down..., just enough to savor life's simple pleasures. At the end of the day, isn't this what it is all about?

Ch. 14: Fatherhood

One of the most challenging and rewarding periods of a husband's life is when they become a father. I have been blessed to be a father of three children, two sons and a daughter. There are definitely no playbooks when it comes to raising children, especially whilst one is serving their country in the US Military.

Our first son (Nathen) has quite the unique birthdate, it is 1-2-3... as in January 2nd, 2003! As a first time father, that made it very easy for me to remember his birthday (you know how us men can be with remembering birthdays). Sheri and I were in California and I was stationed with Naval Mobile Construction Battalion Forty (Fighting Forty). We were married just over 1 year when we found out Sheri was pregnant with our first child.

That feeling of joy and uncertainty one gets as a first time dad is indescribable. We always feel like we are "ready" but when that news hits, we are always a bit taken back and start to think if we truly are *"ready"*. But for those of us who are strong in faith, we understand that even if we think we are not ready, God knows we are and that is why he blessed us with a child.

Nathen took the brunt of my military service. He was the one who was exposed to the numerous deployments when I was with Naval Mobile Construction Battalion Forty. Although he was very young, he felt it was his responsibility to look after Sheri while I was deployed. This made him grow up quickly and gave him a strong sense of duty at a very early age.

He was also old enough to remember all of my time in the military and all the experiences we shared as a family. It was not easy on him. He constantly moved out of state (overseas even) and always had to meet new friends at new schools. This is something I do not think is spoke about enough with military children. With all the moves and new schools, their resilience and adaptability is nothing to shake a stick at! The constant moving and having to meet new friends every few years, hell, this is not easy for adults let alone children! But Nathen always took it in stride and never had issue with meeting new friends, no matter where in the world we were living.

Nathen has grown into a mature, responsible and caring adult. All through High School he was with a few choirs and was a part of an awesome A-capella group. He is extremely talented in the performing and musical arts.

Oh, and he knows just about everything there is to know about the NFL, especially Da Bears!

Our second son, Luke, was born before we transferred to Frankfurt, Germany with the US Department of State. Sheri and Nathen were living in Illinois while I was attending technical training for Department of State in Washington, DC. I had just completed my training when the time was nearing for Luke to be born. I was able to come to Chicago for his birth, I was grateful for this. Actually, I am extremely grateful that for both of my sons (whom were born while I was serving) I was able to be there for their arrival into this world. As many servicemembers can attest, this does not happen often.

Luke is my "mini-me" in just about every aspect. He is quiet and keeps to himself, but has deep thoughts. And when he does speak his thoughts, most times I am taken back by his creativity and intelligence in how he views the world. He also has the musical gene within our family as he plays violin and plays it well! He is going to go far, that is for sure.

I want to explain a bit more about what happened after Luke was born because it was a very trying time for me. Soon after Luke was born, I had to transfer to Frankfurt, Germany. Unfortunately, the family could not go with me right away because their Diplomatic Passports were still being processed. So I had to move to Frankfurt on my own. This was my exposure to being a geographical bachelor and honestly, I hated it!

In the military, there are many who choose to be a geographical bachelor. What this means is, for whatever reason, the servicemember transfers to a new command but their spouse (and children if applicable) stay behind. There are also times where it is not a choice, but rather a necessity due to various reasons. But for my situation, it was an outcome of a process that was taking a little while to get completed (obtaining Diplomatic Passports).

When I arrived to Frankfurt, Germany I will admit, I was an emotional wreck. I had to leave Sheri, Nathen and our newborn baby Luke behind while I flew not to another state, but another country!

When I reported to Frankfurt, I was lonely, plain and simple. Although I had deployed numerous times and was separated from family before, this was different. I really do not know why, but this separation was extremely emotional for me. I was depressed, very depressed. But I carried on.

I got our apartment set up, cable turned on and cellphones activated. We stayed in touch the best we could with the time difference and all, but it just was not the same as having my family with me. I could not wait until they got their Diplomatic passports and would be able to join me in Deutschland. After about a 5 month period, Sheri and the boys finally received their passports and traveled to Germany, what a relief!

For Luke, since he was so young, he does not remember too much from our time in Europe. However, he does have some memories and every once inawhile he will recall a few of them, which is pretty cool. He does say he wants to go back to Germany sometime.... who knows what the future holds!

Gianna is my youngest, she was born after my time in service. I spoke about Gianna's birth in a previous chapter so I will not say to much here. But, she is my one and only daughter and our father-daughter bond is strong! I do not think any father can truly explain what happens when they have a daughter, it is just a totally different feeling of emotion.

But one thing I will speak about in having a daughter is our responsibility as a father. It is our duty to show them how a woman should be treated by a man, plain and simple. I do not always get this right myself, but I will say that how I treat Sheri, it is observed by Gianna. And if I show Sheri disrespect or demean her in any way, Gianna will think that is how a man is supposed to treat her. That is not the example I want to show her! And I believe that any self-respecting father feels the same way when it comes to raising a daughter. Please do not get me wrong, it is equally important to show our son/s how to be a man and a husband as well. But with daughters, I feel that responsibility is taken up a few notches. It really does involve one to "man up", in all respects.

And trust me, I have not forgotten my own upbringing with a "father" who abused my mom. Although I have no sisters, seeing that type of "man" is something I have never forgotten. I try like hell to ensure I do not ever replicate any of those bullshit traits with my own children. As they say, you have to break the cycle if you want to instill a change.

So for me, fatherhood is a ever-evolving learning journey. I do not think there is any one way to raise our children because our specific family dynamics come into play. But there are some fundamentals I believe can be applied across the board, they are as follows:

Show and give love. I will admit, my entire upbringing no one ever said "I love you". I never heard it, period. It was not until I met Sheri that I started feeling "comfortable" saying I love you to my children. I know, this seems crazy, but when you are raised in a family that never says it, you would be amazed how hard it is to say it when you get older.

Raise your children in faith. Read the Bible, go to church, and teach them to have empathy.

Instill discipline. No matter what is happening in the world, I still feel strongly that children need discipline. Discipline cannot be delegated, it needs to start *in the home!*

Teach tithing and servitude. In so doing, you will teach your children to think of others before themselves. In today's world of "look at me" social media, it is more important than ever to show our children how to think and put others ahead of themselves. And when you have been blessed with abundance, it is always wise practice to share that abundance with those less fortunate then you.

Be present. I admit, this is my biggest struggle as a parent. I was raised by a workaholic step-father and I still struggle with work-life balance myself. It does not help that I am in a high operational tempo profession where it requires me to be available 24/7/365. I know I have to do better at being present for my kids. There are times I get so wrapped up in work that when they need me, I just am not there for them. But, this is something we owe to our children. We chose to bring them into this world, the least we can do is be there for them when they need us.

Being a father is a blessing that not everyone gets to enjoy. Do not take it for granted and do not forget the immense amount of responsibility we have as fathers to ensure we raise our children smartly. We only have one chance to get it right.

***

I want to end this book with a few thoughts. I had a few epiphanies as I wrote this book and thought it would be good to share:

- Take time for yourself, your family and your friends. Work will always be there, your friends and family may not. I know this sounds cliche but it is so true.

- Learn to see the good in others. There is a lot of negativity and division in the world today and it is easy to get caught up in it. Filter out the noise and focus on the positive.

- Lead with love just as God commands. Too many business leaders are still too focused on the bottom line and not enough on the people and building relationships. Maybe I am old school but I still believe if you take care of your employees and customers, everything else will fall into place. And the way you do that is with empathy, understanding and mutual respect.

- Find joy. It has seemingly become rare to see people laughing and smiling as they go about their day. And I will admit, I need to do better at this myself. I get pretty grumpy when the pressures of work and life get high and that is not the perception I want to put out to the world. I have the most beautiful wife and children, I really have no reason to be grumpy all the damn time! The way I see it, it is disrespectful to my family to walk around with a grumpy face as it puts out the perception that I am miserable. How can I be when I have been blessed with such a wonderful family?! So, if you too sometimes find yourself being grumpy, try like hell to "turn that frown upside down" and be grateful for all that is around you.., family, friends, and God's grace.

Above all else, find ways to serve others! It is with an attitude of servitude that we all can do our part to make this world a little bit better for all whom inhabit it.

Words of Wit

At the time of this writing, I am age 51. I thought it was a good time to pass on some short tidbits of wisdom:

1. Be *Humble*.
2. Define *Who* you Are
3. *Master* Parallel Parking
4. *Smile*
5. *ABN*… Always Be Networking
6. *ABL*… Always Be Learning
7. Be *Curious*
8. *Confidence* Not *Arrogance*
9. Do Your *Own* Research
10. *Return* Your Grocery Cart
11. Have A *Fondness* For The Arts (any form)
12. ***Do Not Be A Jerk***

Acknowledgements

To my family; Sheri, Nathen, Luke, and Gianna. Words cannot express the love I have for you. I may not always get it right, but I hold you all in my heart, always. You are my lifeblood, you are what keeps me headed forward, you make me whole. Thank you for your support during my military career and your continued support post-Seabees while I adjusted to civilian life, bouncing from job to job until I finally figured things out. And finally, thank you for supporting me on this book writing journey, it was definitely an experience!

I would be remiss if I did not formally thank *you*, *the reader,* for your interest in my book. I also want to thank everyone I ever had the blessing to work with, interact with, be friends with, and make memories with. Especially all my Seabee Brothers and Sisters whom I had the pleasure of serving with to defend our Great Nation against all enemies, foreign and domestic. You all are some of our Nation's finest, do not ever forget that! Stay proud and *tell your story.... America needs to hear it!*

Above all else, I am grateful to God for giving me so much. I am truly living a blessed life.

About The Author

Randy Niznick is a devoted husband, dad and retired United States Navy Seabee (US Naval Construction Force). He served for 23 years, from 1990 to 2013, and was selected to the esteemed rank of Chief Petty Officer in 2004. Randy made a total of eight deployments throughout his military career and supported two Humanitarian / Disaster Recovery Missions. During the last five years of his military service, he was assigned to the Naval Support Unit US Department of State, Diplomatic Security. He and his family lived abroad in Frankfurt, Germany for 3 years while assigned to the State Department and had a follow-on assignment with the Naval Support Unit in Washington, DC for his final 2 years of service in the Navy Seabees.

Upon retiring from the Navy Seabees in 2013, Randy entered corporate life and learned many hard lessons throughout his transition from the military to civilian sector. Randy currently works in Corporate Real Estate (CRE) / Facilities Management (FM) services, specifically supporting critical environments (data center, call center) facilities infrastructure. He is an avid user of LinkedIn and posts about military transition lessons learned, data center opportunities, and CRE / FM services opportunities. He is also a military veteran mentor. Now that he has settled into corporate life and has a number of years working in corporate under his belt, he pays it forward to his fellow Sisters and Brothers and helps them navigate their own transition from the military to civilian sector.

Randy holds a Bachelor of Science in Environmental Management from The University of Maryland Global Campus. He is also a Certified Data Center Practitioner (CDP) and a Facilities Management Professional (FMP).

On the personal side, Randy enjoys cooking, gardening, the outdoors and playing the drums. He loves music (almost any genre) and avidly claims that *smooth jazz is not old man music!*

Randy has been happily married (at the time of publishing this book) for 22 years to his beautiful wife Sheri. They are raising three beautiful children and happily reside in a suburb west of Chicago, Illinois. Ironically, it is in this little town that the man who is known as the "Father of Flag Day" had lived and worked. It is a very patriotic town and being a veteran, this was really the perfect community to plant roots post-Seabees. It is the Niznick family dream to one day own a farmhouse on a large plot of land with horses and maybe some chickens! But until then, they enjoy spending time together and not having to worry about that next deployment.

You can follow or connect with the Author via his LinkedIn profile at: http://linkedin.com/in/rniznick

Disclaimer

I am not a historian. All stories related to the Navy, the Navy Seabees and the US Department of State, Diplomatic Security Service are my personal recollections and do not reflect the US Navy, US Navy Seabees or the US Department of State and their officially documented history.

References

Joint Task Force 160, Operation Sea Signal: https://apps.dtic.mil/sti/pdfs/ADA394323.pdf

Operation Unified Assistance: https://media.defense.gov/2016/Apr/08/2002657496/-1/-1/1/160408-N-ZY182-11824.pdf

Desert Storm/Shield: https://www.history.navy.mil/browse-by-topic/wars-conflicts-and-operations/middle-east/shield-storm.html

Annapolis Peace Conference: President Bush Attends Annapolis Conference (archives.gov)

My Military Career Timeline

1990-1991: Recruit Training Command (Boot Camp)
Great Lakes, IL

1991-1992: USS Elrod, FFG-55
Charleston, SC
Deployment: Desert Storm/Shield (Persian Gulf)

1992: Utilitiesman "A" School
Gulfport, MS

1992-1995: NMCB 74
Gulfport, MS
Deployments: Puerto Rico; Okinawa, Japan (x2); Guantanamo Bay, Cuba

1995-1997: COMNAVACTSUK
London, England

1997-1998: Naval Support Activity
Souda Bay, Crete

1998-2002: Navy Recruiting District Chicago

             Rockford, IL and Des Plaines, IL

2002-2005: NMCB 40
             Pt. Hueneme, CA
             Deployments: Guam; Okinawa, Japan (x2); Banda Aceh, Indonesia

2005-2008: US Naval Academy
             Annapolis, MD

2008-2011: NSU State Department
             Frankfurt, Germany

2011-2013: NSU State Department
             Washington, DC

My Military Retirement Speech Manuscript

I kept a copy of my retirement speech all these years because every once in a while I like to read it and reflect on what I said way back when. It is amazing that as the years have passed (I spoke this speech in August of 2013) much of what I said back then still applies today. So I figured what the heck, why not slip this little diddy into my book!

Speech manuscript:

Well here we are...., 23 years from the day I shipped to boot camp. I cannot believe the day has come to hang up my uniform and don my suit for the next chapter of life. This career has been rewarding and I have learned much from colleagues, friends, family and fellow Chiefs that I know will only help me succeed in the "after life". I thank everyone for being here today to share in my retirement ceremony, it means so much to know how very blessed I am with all of you.

Well, let's get on with it.., shall we?

To the troops/sailors:

The Navy is going through a serious period of societal change, everything from resetting training at the schoolhouses to changing how the training of our new Chief's is to be accomplished. We are now embracing same sex partnerships and truly setting up an organization of Equal Opportunity for all. It is tough to change, but change is necessary to keep things in perspective and moving forward and upward. As leaders and followers we must embrace the change and move forward with it, it will only make our Navy better for future generations. Do not be short-sighted, think long range.....10 to 20 years from now and how what we are doing today will affect the Navy of the future.

Advance youself:

I cannot stress this enough, everyone should get a 4-year degree... period. The civilian job market is competitive as all hell, and being a veteran it is even that much harder to sell yourself to civilians. We all know the Navy is still downsizing, at anytime you can be given your pink slip and told to walk...are you doing everything you can now to ensure you are not another unemployed veteran statistic?

But before you partake in your college endeavors, you need to first seriously think about what it is you really want to do in life post-military.

Dream Big:

When you are alone and with no outside influences...what do you dream about? Where do you see yourself in 10 to 20 years? What are your actual job interests? Many of us just picked a rate because that was what was given to us at the MEPS and we just went with it. Is your current rate what you want to do when you retire/separate from service or do you have other ambitions? Only you know in your heart of hearts what drives you to succeed. Figure out what that is, then find the degree that will help you achieve your success.

Do not get caught up in the LaDR or other tools in the Navy...they may not be for you. Almost all of us in the Seabees are told to get our construction management degree, but is construction what you want to do when you get out? I recently completed my environmental management degree... not much related to being a UT but it is related to what I want to get involved with post-retirement...corporate sustainability. You have to know what it is you really want out of life and then set yourself up for success through education and networking.

Lastly, dream big and big things will happen! I truly

believe this in my heart of hearts... you only limit yourself by your own thoughts and actions. Do not be your own worst enemy.

My choice to retire one year earlier than originally planned was a complete leap of faith. Although I have a strong network and have been involved with civilian institutions, I was not actively looking for work. But I put my trust in God and took this leap of faith (much to the opposition of my wife... she totally freaked out when I called her and said "I'm retiring").

But I can honestly say that thus far this has been the most stress-free transition I could have hoped for. And we have a lot going on with our lives right now... but I always believe it is not our timing but God's timing... you just have to roll with it.
Sometimes you have to take risks in life to achieve your ultimate dreams....do not be afraid to take that leap of faith Seabees!

Market youself:

Everyone of you is a leader. You all have been blessed to be able to lead others, do not ever forget that. And do not ever forget what that truly means... you have the power to influence others...I pray you all use that power for the betterment of others and not for self-gratification. As our new MCPON says "be good to one another".

There are many technicians in the civilian world who never get to lead people...I think they are missing out on a great satisfaction. Think about it... when you see that E-3 put on his or her crow for the first time and you mentored them along the way...doesn't that make you feel good? It should. If it doesn't then you need to get out of the military and find something else to do.

Everyone you meet is a potential network opportunity. Take advantage of that and tell them who you are and what your skills are. You never know who they know...

Now I am not telling everyone to jump ship and get out of the Navy....on the contrary, I want to see all of you have a successful career and advance. But you always have to be thinking about post-Navy life...do not wait until the last minute to prepare.

Life in itself is a continuous preparation, is it not?
Do not get caught up in the Navy bubble....always read civilian trade magazines, get a LinkedIn account, join groups of your career interest and be active in them. Lastly, stay educated on civilian trends in your choice of career. Civilians use different terminology that you may or may not understand. For example, what is the difference between soft skills and hard skills? When do you highlight your soft skills and when do you highlight your hard skills on a resume? You need to think about all this now... do not wait!

Your family:

To those whom are married, respect your spouse at all times. This life is not easy and we ask a lot of our spouses just the same. My beautiful wife Sheri has moved with me and our family 11 times and has been through numerous deployments and TDY's..., it is not an easy thing for them to deal with. You must never forget how much your spouses and children sacrifice so you can serve your Country Honorably. Cherish the time you have together because you never know when you will be deployed again and for how long. And the old line of "what goes on during deployment stays on deployment" is a bunch of bullshit in my opinion. No one should ever be unfaithful to their spouse. It only undermines you as a person but also undermines your authority as a leader of your troops.

The troops you lead:

Never give up on those you are blessed to lead.

Seabees, let me tell you...people can change. Do not ever get into the mindset of "there is no hope for that Seabee"..you cannot fail your troops, ever...

I have enjoyed my time in NSU and most certainly have enjoyed my 23 year Naval Career, and I will undoubtedly miss the camaraderie and the privilege of leading troops. Leadership in the civilian world is a lot different then it is in the military. As crazy as it sounds, I am even going to miss those O'dark-thirty calls from my Seabees asking for advice or needing to talk about personal issues.

That is when you know you are doing it right... when your troops feel completely comfortable talking to you at anytime day or night when they have serious issues going on or just need some career advice. Do not blow them off!!

But it is time for this Old Goat to part ways and close this chapter in the book of life.

Stay proud Seabees and continue to do the great things you all were put on this earth to do. Strive to make a positive impact in someone's life daily and always develop yourself above and beyond your own expectations.

God Bless.

Made in United States
Orlando, FL
12 July 2024